# YOUNG STUDENTS
# World Atlas

NEWFIELD
PUBLICATIONS

SHELTON · CONNECTICUT

# HAMMOND

# DISCOVERING MAPS

Alma Graham - Project Educational Editor

Robert Thomas - Hammond Cartographic Editor

HAMMOND INCORPORATED   MAPLEWOOD, NEW JERSEY

# INTRODUCTION

Suppose you are an explorer, setting forth for a place you have never seen. Will your adventure take you across seas, over land, or into space? Will you have to find your way over broad plains or through thick forests? Will there be treacherous rivers of mud or ice along the way? Perhaps you will have to cross deserts in the scorching sun with little or no water. What if ranges of mountains rise in the distance to block your path? Can you find the best way to get over them before the snow falls?

To succeed in your quest and come safely home, you will have to plan and prepare. What supplies should you carry? An old explorer says that one tool will serve you better than any other. No, it is not a weapon. It is advance knowledge of where you are going. Using it wisely, you can see what lies ahead.

It is a book of maps.

A small map you hold in your hand can show you the world at a single glance. Other maps can give you detailed knowledge of places you've never seen. In which direction should you travel to reach your goal? How many miles must you go? What kind of land will you pass through: Low or high? Flat or steep? Fields or forests? Grasslands or deserts? Where are the best trails or roads? Are there good, safe harbors for ships? What kinds of weather should you prepare for: Hot or cold? Wet or dry? What kinds of foods might you find along the way? Where will you find settlements of people— places where you can get news and buy supplies? Who claims the lands you will be passing through?

Maps can tell you all these things if you learn how to read them. To say so much in so small a space, mapmakers use a kind of code. This book was written to teach you the basic code of maps. Once you can read a map's symbols, you can unlock its secrets. Then you will be ready to do real detective work with maps. First, you'll learn to identify your own place in time and space. Then you'll be ready to venture out to explore your continent—and your universe. With basic map skills to guide you, who knows what hidden marvels maps might help you find?

Alma Graham

**1994 Edition**

**Credits**
**Design and Layout**
Portia Allen
**Illustrations**
Jael (p. 9, 26–27);
**Photos**
NASA (p. 4);
Air Photographics, Inc.,
Wheaton, Maryland (p. 10)

Published for Newfield Publications by special arrangement with Hammond Incorporated.

Young Students Learning Library and Newfield Publications are federally registered trademarks of Newfield Publications, Inc.

# TABLE OF CONTENTS

# Discovering Maps

4

# YOUR PLACE ON EARTH

## Your Earth

You live on the planet Earth. The picture above shows Earth from outer space. From so far away, you can see that Earth is round. You can even see that it has land and water. How can you tell the land and water apart? Why does Earth look small in the picture?

Like Earth, a **globe** is round. The globe on the right is a model of Earth. It looks like Earth but is much smaller. On a globe, it is easy to tell land from water. You can clearly see the shapes

of the land. You can also see the names people have given to places on Earth.

**1.** A toy train is a model of a railroad train. A doll or action figure is a model of a person. What other models can you name?
**2.** How is the globe like the picture of Earth? How is it different?

## Your Half of Earth

**HALF OF EARTH IS A HEMISPHERE**

**EARTH IS A SPHERE**

Earth is round. It is shaped like a ball. Something ball-shaped can be called a globe or **sphere**. Half a sphere is a **hemisphere**. Hemi- means "half" in Greek. So a hemisphere is our name for half of Earth.

## Your Hemispheres

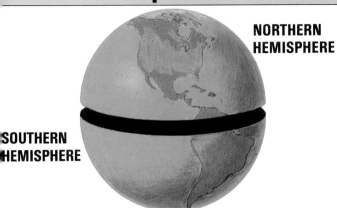

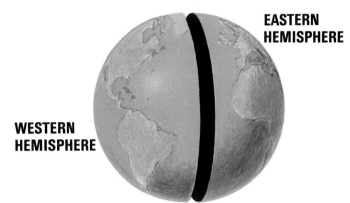

We can divide Earth into a northern half and a southern half. You live in the northern half of Earth. So you live in the **Northern Hemisphere**. Or, we can divide Earth into an eastern half

and a western half. You live in the western half of Earth. So you live in the **Western Hemisphere.**

## Earth's Land and Water

Look at a globe that you can turn. How much of Earth can you see at one time? Why?

Earth has seven large areas of land called **continents**. Asia, Africa, North America, South America, Antarctica, Europe and Australia are continents. They are listed here in order of their size. Asia and Africa are the largest.

Smaller areas of land with water all around them are called **islands**. The islands on the globes below are colored brown. The smallest continent, Australia, is over three times bigger than the largest island, Greenland.

Earth also has four large bodies of water called **oceans**. Find the names of the oceans on the globes below. The four oceans are really part of one huge body of water. In fact, you live in a very watery world. Look at Earth's oceans on a globe. Does planet Earth have more dry land or more water?

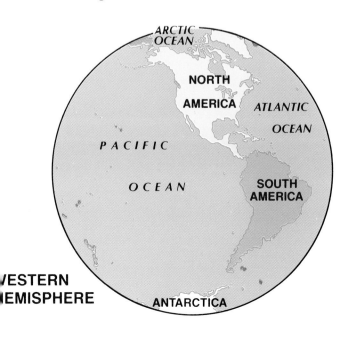

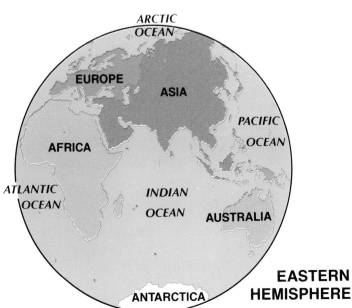

## Your Continent

The globe at the right shows your continent. It is **North America**. Three of Earth's oceans touch North America. They are the Atlantic Ocean, the Pacific Ocean and the Arctic Ocean. Which Ocean does not touch North America? To find out, look at the globes on page 5.

There are ten countries on the continent of North America. A **country** has its own land, people and government. It is also called a **nation**.

Your country is called the **United States of America**. Find the United States on the globe. Find two other large nations of North America.

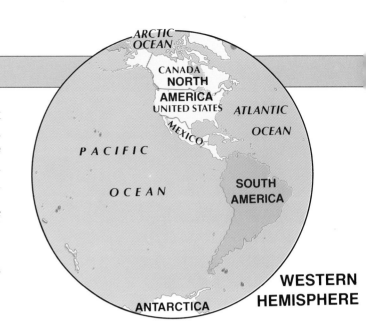

**WESTERN HEMISPHERE**

## Your Country

The United States is made up of 50 parts called **states**. Of these states, 48 touch one another. Two states, Alaska and Hawaii, are separate. Puerto Rico is not a state but is a part of the United States.

Each state has many towns and cities. Each town and city has neighborhoods and schools. Start with your school. Tell where you are on Earth. Where you are is your **location**.

1 – Guatemala
2 – Belize
3 – El Salvador
4 – Honduras
5 – Nicaragua
6 – Costa Rica
7 – Panama

**1.** Suppose you live in the United States of America. But suppose you do not live on the continent of North America. Where do you live? **2.** In what ways does your location change during the day? In what ways does it stay the same?

# FACTS ABOUT OUR EARTH

## Earth Rotates and Gives Us Days

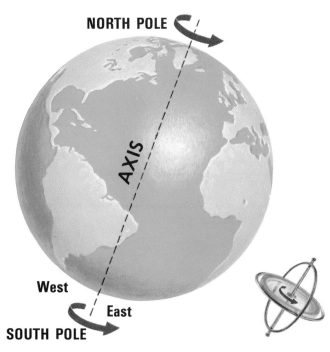

**NORTH POLE**

AXIS

West

East

**SOUTH POLE**

**1 ROTATION = 24 HOURS = 1 DAY**

Earth is a **planet**. A planet is a large solid body that moves around a star. Our star is the sun. Our planet's movements in space help us measure time.

Earth's **axis** is an imaginary line that runs through the center of Earth. The ends of the axis are the **North Pole** and **South Pole**. Earth turns around its axis the way a top spins. To move this way is to **rotate**. We call Earth's movement around its axis **rotation**.

It takes 24 hours for Earth to rotate around its axis. That is why a **day** on Earth is 24 hours long. We have daytime when our part of Earth faces the sun. We have nighttime when our part of Earth faces away from the sun. Daytime and nighttime together make a 24-hour day.

THINK ABOUT IT

On two days a year, the hours of daytime and nighttime are equal. How many hours of daytime do we have then?

## Earth's Rotation Gives Us Directions

Earth's rotation also helps us tell **directions**. The four main directions on Earth are **north**, **south**, **east** and **west**. North and south are defined by Earth's axis. To go **north** means to go toward the North Pole. To go **south** means to go toward the South Pole. East and west are defined by Earth's rotation around its axis. Earth rotates from west to east. That is why the sun seems to rise in the **east** in the morning. That is why the sun seems to set in the **west** at night.

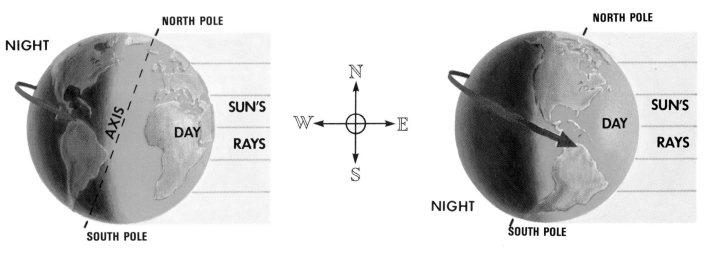

**NIGHT**

**NORTH POLE**

AXIS

**SUN'S**

**DAY**

**RAYS**

N

W ⊕ E

S

**NORTH POLE**

**SUN'S**

**DAY**

**RAYS**

**NIGHT**

**SOUTH POLE**

**SOUTH POLE**

# Earth Revolves and Gives Us Years

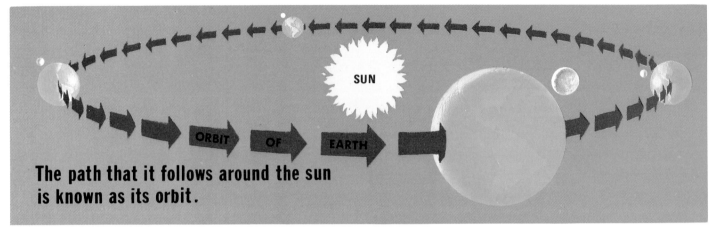

The path that it follows around the sun is known as its orbit.

**1 REVOLUTION = 365 DAYS = 1 YEAR**

Earth also travels, or **revolves**, around the sun. The path Earth takes is called an **orbit**. It takes 365 1/4 days for Earth to make one **revolution**, or trip, around the sun. That is why a **year** on Earth is 365 days long.

 Every four years, we usually have a leap year of 366 days. Why?

# Earth's Position Gives Us Seasons

Why do seasons change on Earth? This happens because Earth revolves around the sun. It also happens because Earth's axis leans to one side. The axis is slanted, or tilted.

In June, the North Pole leans toward the sun. So the northern half of Earth gets more of the sun's light and heat. Because of this, the weather gets warmer. Summer comes to the Northern Hemisphere. The day that spring becomes summer is the day of longest light.

In December, the North Pole leans away from the sun. So the northern half of Earth gets less of the sun's light and heat. As a result, the weather gets colder. Winter comes to the Northern Hemisphere. As winter approaches, it gets dark earlier in the evening. The day that fall becomes winter is the day of shortest light.

In the Southern Hemisphere, seasons are just the opposite. The South Pole is tilted toward the sun in December. It is tilted away from the sun in June. The continent of Australia is in the Southern Hemisphere. When does summer start there?

**1.** In June, the North Pole leans toward the sun. This is a cause. Name one or more effects. **2.** The Northern Hemisphere has winter. This is an effect. What is the cause?

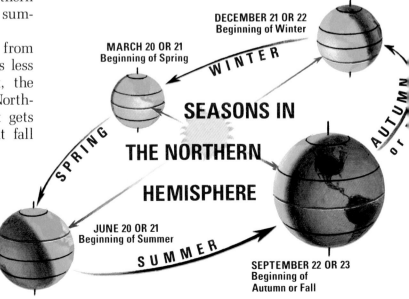

DECEMBER 21 OR 22
Beginning of Winter

MARCH 20 OR 21
Beginning of Spring

WINTER

SEASONS IN

SPRING

THE NORTHERN

AUTUMN or

HEMISPHERE

JUNE 20 OR 21
Beginning of Summer

SUMMER

SEPTEMBER 22 OR 23
Beginning of
Autumn or Fall

## Land of the Midnight Sun

Near the North Pole, the seasons are much different. Because of the tilt of Earth's axis, the sun is never directly overhead. This means the weather is always cold. Winter at the North Pole is a time of darkness, day and night. The sun never rises.

Summer at the North Pole is a time when the sun never sets. You can see the sun even at midnight. That is why the area near the North Pole is called the "land of the midnight sun."

## Your Place in Time and Space

**NORTH POLE**
**POLAR REGION** always cold
NORTH MID-LATITUDE REGION seasons change
TROPICAL REGION
EQUATOR always hot
SOUTH MID-LATITUDE REGION seasons change
**SOUTH POLE**
**POLAR REGION** always cold

at an angle

direct

You live on the third planet from the sun. You live between the middle of the Earth and the North Pole. You know your continent is North America and your country is the United States. You know what day and month and year it is today. You know how many revolutions Earth has made since you were born. As you learn about Earth, you are finding your own special place in time and space.

**THINK ABOUT IT**

1. Look at the globe to the left. Do you live in a part of Earth where seasons change?
2. How many revolutions has Earth made since you were born?

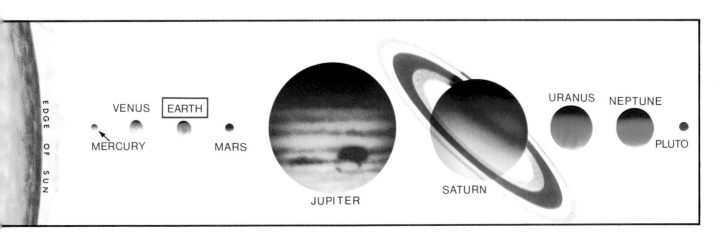

EDGE OF SUN

MERCURY  VENUS  EARTH  MARS  JUPITER  SATURN  URANUS  NEPTUNE  PLUTO

# HOW MAPS SHOW PLACES ON EARTH

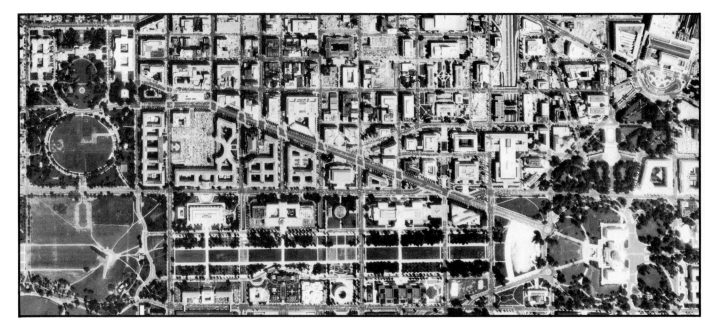

A **map** is a flat drawing of a place or places on Earth. A map can show the whole Earth, as a globe does. Or, a map can show any part of Earth.

A map shows a place from above. It is like a picture taken from high in the air or from outer space. Such a picture is called an **aerial photograph**.

The aerial photograph above shows part of Washington, D.C. This is a view from an airplane. The map opposite it on page 11 is a drawing of the same area.

Today, aerial photographs help mapmakers make better maps. In the past, though, people could not take photographs of Earth from the air. They had to explore a place before they could map it.

An explorer had to sail along a coast to draw a map of the coastline. Explorers had to cross our continent in canoes, on horseback, and on foot. Only then could they draw maps showing what North America was like. They found forest and deserts, lakes and rivers, plains and mountains. They also discovered the best trails to follow. All these features can be shown on maps.

# MAPPING AMERICA: THEN AND NOW

First map showing "America" as a continent: **1507**

Map of Virginia by John Smith: **1612**

Colonist Lewis Evans maps the "Middle British Colonies in America": **1755**

Lewis and Clark explore and map western North America: **1804–1806**

First photograph made: **1826**

First successful airplane flight: **1903**

First artificial Earth satellite launched: **1957**

First Landsat satellite photographs Earth: **1972**

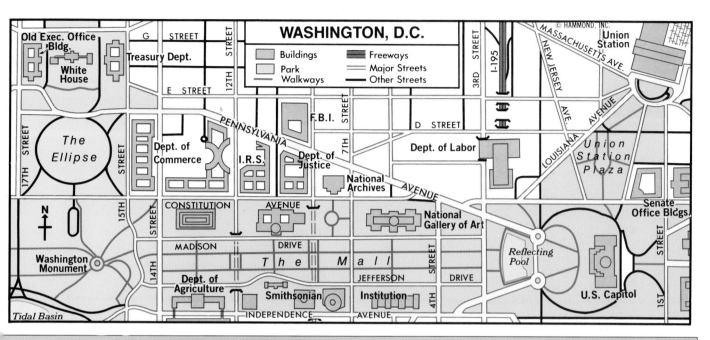

**WASHINGTON, D.C.**

KEY:
- Buildings
- Park
- Walkways
- Freeways
- Major Streets
- Other Streets

© HAMMOND, INC.

# Reading Symbols on Maps

A map has to show a large area in a small space. That is why mapmakers use symbols. A map **symbol** is a drawing or color that stands for a real place or thing. A special section on each map shows what the symbols mean. This section is called the map **key**, or **legend.**

The map above shows Washington, D.C. Look at the map symbols in the key. Find the symbol for buildings. It has a special color. Now find the U.S. Capitol on the map. Then compare that map symbol with the actual Capitol in the aerial photograph on page 10.

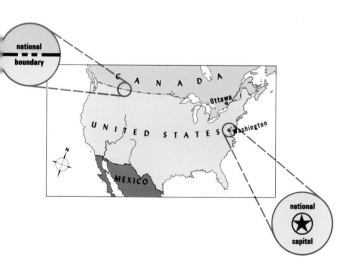

The secrets of each map are locked inside its symbols. Some special symbols appear on many maps. You will find them when you use a book of maps, or **atlas.**

Map symbols may be simple **shapes**, such as a dot or star. On most maps of a large area, a black dot ● stands for a city. Many mapmakers use a star ★ to stand for a state capital. Others show a state capital as a dot in a circle. ⊙ A star in a circle ⊛ usually marks the capital of a country, or a national capital. Washington, D.C., is the capital of the United States. Find it on the map of the United States at the bottom of page 17.

**Lines** are also used as symbols on maps. A line may mark a road or river. Or it

| KEY | |
|---|---|
| National Capital | ⊛ |
| State Capital | ★ |
| Other Cities | ● |
| National Boundary | —— |
| State Boundary | – – – |

may be a **border**, also called a **boundary.** A boundary is a line that separates one city, state or nation from another. Boundaries may be marked by solid lines —— or broken lines — · — · — of dots and dashes.

**1.** In what ways are the map and the photograph alike? In what ways do they differ? **2.** What information does the map give you that the photograph does not? Name as many examples as you can.

# Reading Symbols on Maps (cont'd)

Other symbols are more than lines or shapes. They may be **drawings** that suggest the thing they stand for. Symbols showing natural resources are of this type. A drawing of an oil derrick may show where oil wells are found. Crossed pickaxes may stand for metals that people dig out of the ground.

 Test your powers of **inference**. You may recognize more symbols than you think. Match each map symbol at the left with the thing it stands for on the right.

| SYMBOL | | NAME |
|---|---|---|
| 1. | | a. railroad |
| 2. | | b. airport |
| 3. | | c. river |
| 4. | | d. bridge |
| 5. | | e. mountain |

 **PAST & PRESENT**

In Greek myths of long ago, Atlas was a giant. He was huge and was very strong and powerful. In fact, it was his job to hold up the sky on his shoulders!

Mapmakers four centuries ago knew the old story of Atlas. They put drawings of him in their books of maps. His picture was right on the title page, holding up a globe of the Earth. Because of this, many people today think Atlas held up the whole world—not just the sky. Either way, it must have been a very heavy load!

To this day, a map book is called an atlas. An atlas shows places on Earth. Sometimes an atlas also has a map of the skies.

Maps are easier to read when **colors** are used. Colors are really another kind of symbol. They can tell you many things.

Colors help us tell land from water easily. Usually water is shown by the color blue. Because of this, blue is rarely used to show any other feature. Land can be shown by any other colors.

Colors can also help you tell one state or nation from another. On the map at the right, notice how different colors separate the United States from Canada. Alaska is the same color as the United States. This tells you that Alaska is part of the United States, not part of Canada.

Mapmakers use bright colors to show important information. Look at the road map on Page 31. What types of things are shown in red? Is it easier to see some roads because they are red?

## NORTH AMERICA

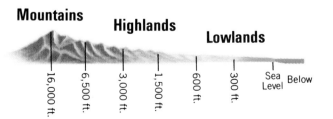

Sometimes map colors show whether land is low and flat, or high and full of mountains. Notice how colors are used on the Alaska map at the left. The brown colors show mountains. Green shows us where the low, flat land is located. Does Alaska have more mountains or lowlands?

Map colors can also show whether lands are hot or cold, rainy or dry, empty or full of people. Make your own map. What will you use colors to show?

What colors would you use to show these kinds of places on a map?

1. cold places

2. warm or hot places

3. dry places

4. mountains

# TELLING DIRECTIONS ON MAPS

Maps have symbols other than those shown in the map key. Every map needs at least one symbol to show direction. A real **compass** is a small magnet. It has a movable needle that always points north. The most common symbol for direction is a straight arrow pointing north. It is called a **direction arrow**.

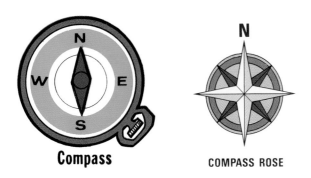

**Compass**          **COMPASS ROSE**

In the past, mapmakers often drew fancy direction arrows. Some of these pointers looked like petals on a rose. So a direction symbol with many pointers came to be called a **compass rose**.

A compass rose is a drawing used on a map. It has an arrow or pointer to show where north is. Often it shows all four **cardinal directions**. These are the four main directions on Earth: north, south, east, and west.

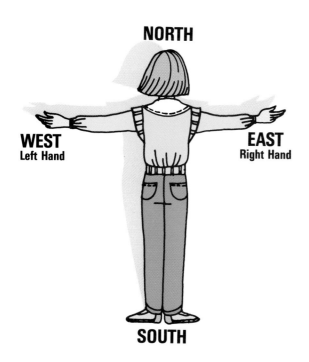

**NORTH**

**WEST**
Left Hand

**EAST**
Right Hand

**SOUTH**

**MAP OF NORTH AMERICA**

Mapmakers abbreviate the cardinal directions. They use the first letter of each word. N stands for north, S for south, E for east, and W for west.

When you know where north is, you can find the other directions. South is opposite north. East is right of north. West is left of north.

There are also **intermediate** ("in-between") **directions**. They help you be more exact in telling where things are located. **Northeast** (NE) is between north and east. **Southwest** (SW) is between south and west. Where is **southeast**? Where is **northwest**?

Some maps show cardinal and intermediate directions on a compass rose. Now you know what this map symbol means.

Mapmakers usually draw maps so that north is at the top of the page. This is not always true, though. Remember: north and south are not the same as up and down. Up means "toward the sky." North means "toward the North Pole."

North and south refer to fixed points on the planet Earth. You cannot go farther south than the South Pole. However, there are no natural stopping points for east and west. You could travel all the way around the Earth by traveling east. If you did this, where would you end up?

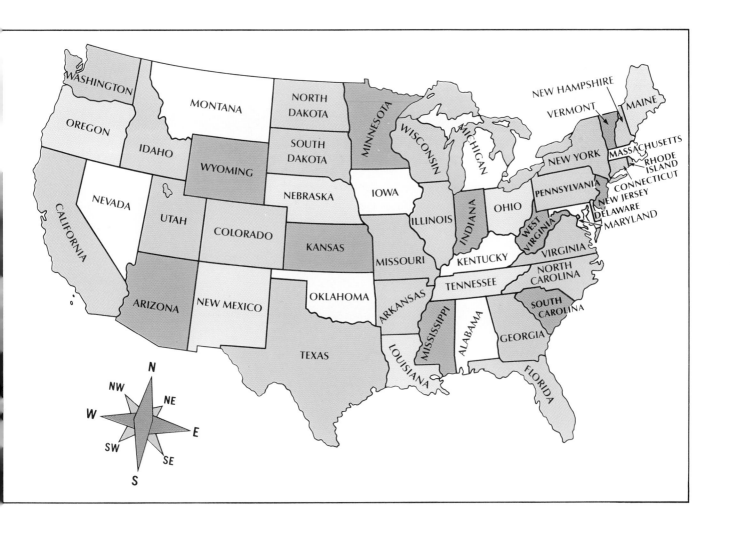

We use map directions in two major ways. We may use them to describe **absolute** (unchanging) **locations**. For example, in the United States, Georgia is in the South. New Jersey is in the East. Arizona is in the Southwest. Oregon is in the Northwest.

We may also use directions to tell **relative** (changing) **locations**. Find Illinois on the map above. If you are in Wisconsin, Illinois is south of you. If you are in Pennsylvania, Illinois is west of you. Illinois is not moving. You are changing your point of view.

Now try using the intermediate directions. To get from Florida to Illinois, you go northwest. To get from Montana to Illinois, which way do you go?

Play a game. Give hints and let someone guess where you are. For example: "To get to Pennsylvania, I go north. To get to Virginia, I go south. To get to West Virginia, I go west. To get to Delaware, I go east. Where am I?"

**1.** Imagine you are in a small round room with windows on all sides. Every window faces south. You see a bear outside. Where are you? What color is the bear? **2.** What are the abbreviations for southeast and northwest? **3.** Lets go for a trip. Use your sense of direction: northeast, northwest, southeast, or southwest? In what direction do we head?

a. From New Jersey to Maine, go _____.

b. From Michigan to New Mexico, go _____.

c. From Georgia to Idaho, go_____.

d. From Wyoming to Louisiana, go _____ .

# MEASURING DISTANCES ON MAPS

Maps not only show you where places are located. They can help you figure out how far one place is from another. When you measure "how far," you are measuring **distance**.

The distance between places on Earth is measured in miles or kilometers. On a map, though, two big cities may be only an inch apart. When you measure distance on a map, you need to change it into real distance on Earth. To do this,

you use a distance scale.

A **distance scale** is a horizontal line or bar on a map. Look at the scale above. One bar shows what the map distance equals in miles. The other shows what the map distance equals in kilometers. The mapmaker lets a small length stand for a larger one. On the map, how far is Atlanta from Miami in inches? How many miles does this stand for?

## Using a Distance Scale

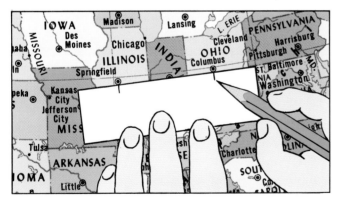

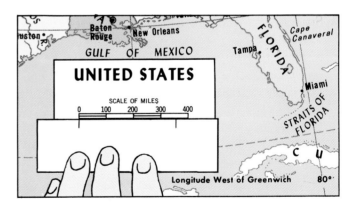

The maps above show you how to measure the distance between two cities. The cities in the sample are state capitals: Springfield, Illinois, and Columbus, Ohio. First, locate the two city dots. Then, mark off the space between them on the edge of a piece of paper. Next, place your paper under the scale of miles on the map. Put the first mark at zero. The second mark falls halfway between 300 and 400. The distance between these cities is about 350 miles.

Next, measure the distance between Spring-

field, Illinois and Harrisburg, Pennsylvania. This time, your marked section is longer than the distance scale. Put your first mark at zero. Add a mark where the scale ends. Label this new mark 400. Then move the 400 mark to zero and start over. What new distance do you get? Add the new distance to 400. What is the total distance in miles? Now practice measuring distance using the map and Scale of Miles on page 16. How far is it from New York to Boston? From Dallas to New Orleans? From Chicago to Atlanta?

17

**1.** Use the map at the top of page 16. What is the map distance from Madison, Wisconsin to Lansing, Michigan?

**2.** Can you drive from Madison to Lansing in a straight line? Why or why not?

**3.** Suppose you went from Springfield, Illinois to Columbus, Ohio by bus. Would the road distance be the same as the map distance? Or would the road distance be longer or shorter? Why?

 In the United States, we use two different systems of measurement. One is called the **customary system**. It measures distances in inches, feet, yards and miles. In olden times, people used parts of their body as standards for measuring. An **inch** was the width of a man's thumb. A **foot** was the length of his foot. A man held out his arm to measure a **yard**. It was the distance from his nose to the tip of his middle finger.

Since people were different sizes, they had to agree on standard measurements. The result was our customary system. In it, 12 inches equal a foot, and 3 feet equal a yard. A **mile** is 5,280 feet.

The more modern system of measurement is the **metric system**. It measures distances in centimeters, meters and kilometers. These are standard sizes based on counting by 10's. One **centimeter** equals 1/100 meter, or 2/5 inch. One **kilometer** equals 1000 meters, or 3/5 mile. Metric measurements are now used around the world.

## Map Scale

A **scale** is a means of measuring something. You stand on a scale to measure your weight. Scale also means the size of one thing compared to another. Map scale lets you compare sizes on a map to sizes on Earth.

The same place can be shown on maps of different sizes. Look at the maps below. The first map shows only the state of California. The second shows California as part of our nation, the United States. The third map shows California's place on the continent of North America. As the area shown on the map gets larger, the map scale gets smaller. California seems to be getting smaller, too. Actually, its real size on Earth remains the same.

Look at the maps of Ohio below. One map shows the whole state. The other shows five cities in the northeastern part of the state. One inch on the map of five cities equals 32 miles. One inch on the state map equals 85 miles.

The map of the larger area—the state—is drawn to a smaller scale. That means that places on the map look smaller. The cities seem closer together. Still, the real distance between the cities has not changed.

Measure the map distance between Cleveland and Canton on the state map above. Use the distance scale. How many miles does this tell you it is? Now, measure the map distance on the five cities map. Use the scale on that map to find out how far it is. What are your answers? Should these answers be the same?

Usually a map of a large area, such as a state or entire nation, must be drawn on a small scale. Not much detail can be shown. For example, on a map of a state, cities may appear as just dots. Rivers may be just a thin line.

A map of a smaller area can be drawn on a larger scale in the same space. More detail can be added. For example, a map of a city or neighborhood may include streets, highways, parks and even important buildings. Rivers may be shown by drawing both banks, and may even include symbols for docks and bridges.

Mapmakers decide what information their maps need to show. Then they choose the best scale to suit the purpose.

You can be a mapmaker too. Plan a map of your room. What scale might you use? Measure your room. Using these measurements, how large would your map be if one inch equals one foot? How large would your map be if one inch equals two feet?

Have you mastered distance measurement? Turn to the map of the United States on page 41. Measure the distances between the following state capitals. Use the scale of miles to change the map distance into real distance on Earth.

1. Sacramento, California to Carson City, Nevada
2. Denver, Colorado to Santa Fe, New Mexico
3. Des Moines, Iowa to Pierre, South Dakota
4. Atlanta, Georgia to Columbia, South Carolina
5. Albany, New York to Augusta, Maine

# FINDING LOCATIONS ON MAPS

Have you ever given directions in a neighborhood? You often refer to crossing streets, or **intersections**. Mapmakers can create intersections for you on maps by using crossing lines. To see how this works, look at the map of Pennsylvania on the right. The mapmaker has drawn lines from top to bottom and from side to side. These crossing lines divide the map into a pattern of squares called a **grid**.

Now look around all four sides of the map. The letters A, B, C and D go across the top and bottom. The numbers 1, 2, 3 and 4 go down both sides. Thus, each square in the grid has both a letter and a number. The letter and the number are the address of the square.

Find square C-3. First, at the top of the map, find the letter C. Then, at the side of the map, find the number 3. Move one finger down column C. Move another finger across row 3. Your fingers will meet at square C-3. The capital of Pennsylvania is there. What is it?

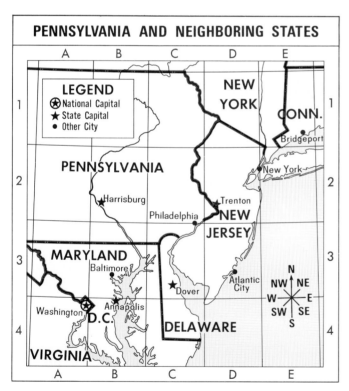

Now find square A-1. It includes Pennsylvania's northwestern boundary. What city is in square A-1? Now find square A-3. It is in southwestern Pennsylvania. What city is in square A-3? Pennsylvania's largest city is in square D-4. What is it?

Have you ever tried to locate a place by looking in an atlas? A map index makes places easy to find. A **map index** is an alphabetical listing of place names on a map or maps. For each place name in the atlas, it gives a page number and a grid square.

Look at the map of Pennsylvania and neighboring states. Suppose you are in Dover, Delaware. You want to find Bridgeport, Connecticut. Use the index below the map. In what square is Dover? Find it on the map. In what square is Bridgeport? To get from Dover to Bridgeport, which way would you go?

 How many state capitals are shown on the map on the left? List each state capital and its grid location.

## PENNSYLVANIA AND NEIGHBORING STATES

| | |
|---|---|
| Annapolis . . . . . . . . . . . . B 4 | Harrisburg . . . . . . . . . . . B 2 |
| Atlantic City . . . . . . . . . . D 3 | New York . . . . . . . . . . . . E 2 |
| Baltimore . . . . . . . . . . . . B 3 | Philadelphia . . . . . . . . . . C 2 |
| Bridgeport . . . . . . . . . . E 1 | Trenton . . . . . . . . . . . . D 2 |
| Dover . . . . . . . . . . . . . . C 3 | Washington . . . . . . . . . . A 4 |

| CAPITAL | GRID LOCATION |
|---|---|
| _____ | _____ |
| _____ | _____ |
| _____ | _____ |
| _____ | _____ |

# LATITUDE AND LONGITUDE

To find a place exactly, you need crossing lines that create an intersection. This is a grid system. One grid system is used by mapmakers all over the world. It helps you locate any place on Earth. It is known as the latitude and longitude grid.

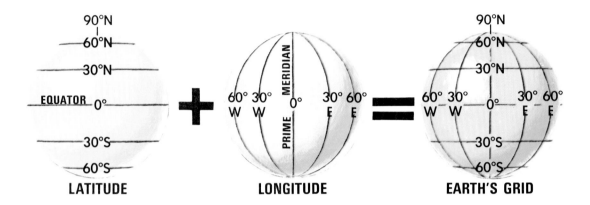

LATITUDE + LONGITUDE = EARTH'S GRID

# Latitude

Halfway between the North Pole and the South Pole is an imaginary line, the **equator**. The equator goes around the middle of Earth like a belt. It divides our planet into the Northern Hemisphere and the Southern Hemisphere.

The equator is a line of **latitude**. The other lines of latitude are north and south of the equator. They are parallel to the equator. Parallel lines run in the same direction and are an equal distance apart at all points. They never meet. Thus, lines of latitude are also called **parallels**. They run east-west around the globe.

Parallels measure distance north or south of the equator. This distance is measured in **degrees**. Earth, as a circle, is divided into 360 degrees (360°).

We measure latitude starting at the equator. Its address is zero degrees latitude, or 0° latitude. The distance from the equator to the North Pole is 1/4 of the distance around the Earth. So the North Pole is at 90 degrees north latitude. The distance from the equator to the South Pole is also 1/4 of the distance around the Earth. What is the latitude of the South Pole?

You can measure your latitude by using the night sky. In the Northern Hemisphere, find the North Star, Polaris. Extend one arm toward the star. Extend your other arm toward the horizon. The **horizon** is the point where the sky and land seem to meet in the distance.

Use a protractor to measure the number of degrees between your outstretched arms. If the angle is 40 degrees, you are located at 40° north. At the equator, Polaris appears right at the horizon. You are at 0° latitude.

What latitude do you find if you try this? How close is this to an accurate figure found in an atlas?

# Longitude

Another set of imaginary lines helps us measure distance east and west. These are lines of **longitude**. Each line of longitude runs from the North Pole to the South Pole. These lines are also called **meridians**.

Each meridian travels halfway around the Earth. Along its imaginary journey it crosses each line of latitude once. These intersections mark an exact location for any point on Earth.

Longitude lines are measured in degrees, just as latitude. However, there is no natural starting or stopping point for east and west. So mapmakers need a place to begin. They call that line of longitude the **prime meridian**. Its address is zero degrees longitude, or 0° longitude.

From the prime meridian, you can travel west halfway around the Earth to the 180° west longitude line. You may also travel east halfway around the Earth to the 180° east longitude line. At the 180° line, east meets west: 180° E and 180° W are the same line!

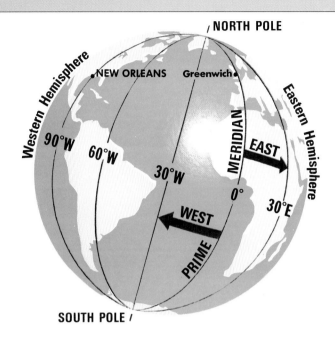

Look at the globe above. Notice that lines of longitude do not stay the same distance from each other. Meridians are farthest apart at the equator. They are closer together at the poles.

In fact, one degree east-west is 69 miles at the equator. At the poles there is no distance between each degree line. They all meet at the same spot!

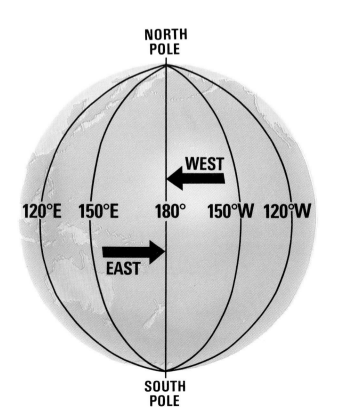

**PAST & PRESENT** Today, the prime meridian passes through Greenwich, England, part of the city of London. But it wasn't always so.

Until the 19th century, mapmakers would place the zero degree line wherever they wished. Often it was shown running through the capital city of the nation where they lived. Paris was the location of the prime meridian for French mapmakers. Rome was at zero degrees longitude for Italian mapmakers.

In 1884, 25 nations finally agreed on the **Greenwich Meridian**. In time, mapmakers of other countries also began using that line as zero degrees longitude.

However, if the Greenwich Meridian is used to divide Earth into Eastern and Western Hemispheres, the continents of Europe and Africa are partly in both hemispheres. For this reason, even now, some mapmakers would like to move the location of the prime meridian.

You can use parallels and meridians to write addresses for any place on Earth. The map at the right shows the address of New Orleans, Louisiana. How would you write this address?

Find the global address of Philadelphia, Pennsylvania on the map below. Philadelphia is at 40° north latitude and 75° west longitude. These numbers and directions are the **coordinates** of Philadelphia. So, 40° N, 75° W is the address of the intersection on Earth at which Philadelphia is found.

To find the coordinates of Trenton, New Jersey on the map below, a longer address is needed. Each degree of latitude and longitude may be divided into sixty **minutes**. The address for Trenton is 40 degrees, 13 minutes north latitude and 74 degrees, 45 minutes west latitude. This is written: 40° 13′ N, 74° 45′ W.

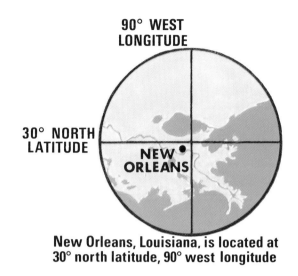

New Orleans, Louisiana, is located at 30° north latitude, 90° west longitude

## Latitude Affects Climate

The latitude of a place affects its **climate**, or usual pattern of weather. Areas near the equator remain hot all year. Lands near the North Pole and South Pole are usually cold.

In between the equator and the poles is an area of changing seasons. This area is called the **mid-latitudes**. Here, in the Northern Hemisphere, warm summers arrive in the middle of the year. Colder winters begin as the year ends. In the Southern Hemisphere, these seasons are just the opposite.

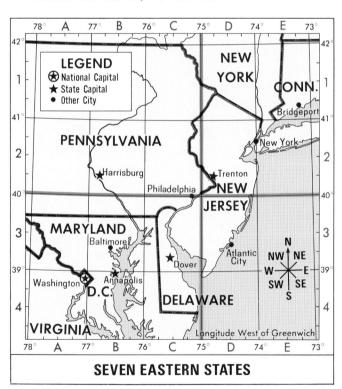

SEVEN EASTERN STATES

**1.** How would you write the address for New Orleans, Louisiana in degrees and minutes? **2.** Use the map above. What city is at 39° N, 77° W? **3.** If you were standing in New Orleans at night, how many degrees above the horizon would you have to extend your arm to point to the North Star, Polaris?

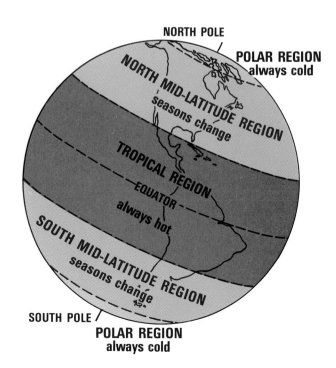

# TIME ZONES

Because Earth rotates, some places have daylight while other places have darkness. Wherever you are, it is noon when the sun is at its highest point overhead. However, noon and lunchtime for you may be sunset and suppertime for someone in Europe.

We need to know what time it is all over the world. To do this, we have divided Earth into **time zones**. It is the same time at any place in the same time zone. Each day is 24 hours long. Each time zone represents one hour. How many time zones does Earth have?

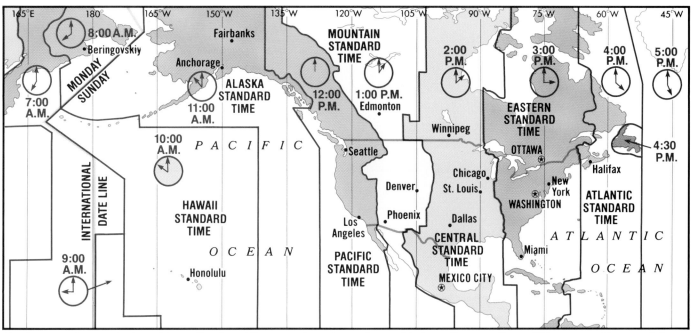

No time zone is exactly 15° wide at all points. The zones have been changed to keep the same time within many nations or states.

# Longitude Affects Time Zones

Just as latitude affects climate, longitude affects time. In fact, the word meridian means "midday", or "noon." When the sun is directly above a meridian, it is noon there. Our abbreviations **A.M.** and **P.M.** mean "before noon" and "after noon."

Divide Earth's 360° by the 24 hours in a day. You will get 15°. Each time zone is about 15° of longitude in width.

Earth rotates from west to east. Thus a day starts and ends first in the east. So when you enter a new time zone going west, what happens to the time?

For most of its length, the 180th meridian forms the **International Date Line**. This is an imaginary line marking the spot where a new calendar day starts. On the east longitude side of the line, it is one day later than on the west longitude side. Thus, when you cross this line, you gain or lose a whole day!

Use the time zone map above.
**1.** You are having supper in New York at 6:00 P.M. For your friend, it is only 1:00 P.M. and lunchtime. In what state does your friend live? **2.** You are in Miami, Florida. A friend in Los Angeles, California phones you at 4:00 P.M. Pacific Time. What time is it in Miami when you get the call? **3.** It is noon in Seattle, Washington. What time is it in these places?

    a. Phoenix, Arizona
    b. St. Louis, Missouri
    c. Washington, D.C.
    d. Fairbanks, Alaska
    e. Honolulu, Hawaii

**4.** When it is 10:00 A.M. Sunday in Honolulu, Hawaii, what time is it in Beringovskiy?

# POLITICAL MAPS

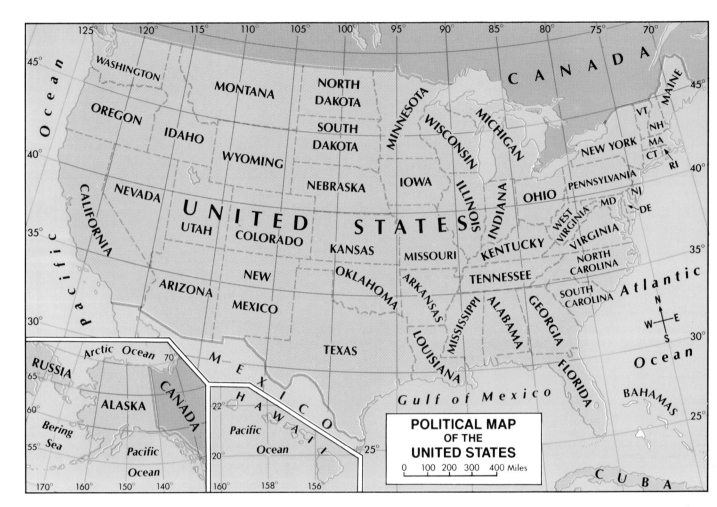

POLITICAL MAP
OF THE
UNITED STATES
0   100 200 300   400 Miles

A **political map** shows the lines that divide one nation, state, county or city from another. These are **political boundaries**. People set political boundaries, and people can change them.

The map above is a political map of the United States. The United States is made up of 50 states. Of these, 48 states are **contiguous**, or touch each other. The 49th state, Alaska, touches Canada's northwest border. The 50th state, Hawaii, is near the middle of the Pacific Ocean.

## Political Map Insets

On maps of the United States, Alaska and Hawaii are often shown in boxes called **insets**. Both states are too far away from the others to be shown at an accurate distance on the main map. Separating these states in an inset is one way to let us know that.

Find the Alaska inset on the map above. Notice that Alaska is drawn to a smaller scale than the main map. Alaska is really the largest state and the one farthest north. You can see its relative size and position on the North America map on page 25.

Insets are often used to show more detail in a crowded area. By drawing the inset at a larger scale, the mapmaker can include more information. Areas around large cities where there are many towns are often shown this way.

1. On the map above, is the Hawaii inset drawn at a smaller or larger scale than the main map? 2. Which state is farthest south? How can you tell on the map above? 3. Which state is farthest west?

# Political Map Symbols

The key to a political map may show the symbols used for political boundaries and capital cities. The **capital** of a state or nation is the city where the central government is located. The capital of the United States is not in any state. It is in a federal district, the District of Columbia, or D.C.

The map on the right is a political map of North America. On this map, different colors show where one nation stops and another starts. Lines are also drawn on the map to serve as symbols for national boundaries.

Find the capital of Canada on the map of North America. Then, name the national capital located at 20° north latitude, 100° west longitude. Can you give the latitude and longitude location of Washington, D.C.?

Next, find Puerto Rico on the main map and in the large scale inset. Puerto Rico is not a state. It is a separate part of the United States. Puerto Ricans are citizens of the United States.

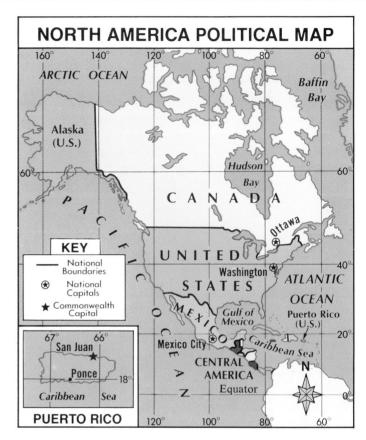

# More About Political Boundaries

Some political boundaries follow the curving lines of coasts, rivers or mountains. Others are straight lines marked on maps but invisible in the real world. Often, straight boundaries follow lines of latitude or longitude.

You can find examples of these kinds of boundaries on the map to the right. It shows the Southeastern states. Notice the irregular eastern boundaries of the states on the Atlantic coast. Then find the line of 35° north latitude. It forms the entire southern boundary of Tennessee. What three states have this 35th parallel as their northern boundary?

**1.** If you take a trip from one state to another, would you see the boundary lines as you cross them? What if the boundary line were the same as a river? **2.** How might you tell when you leave one state and enter another? **3.** How would you tell when you left one country and entered another?

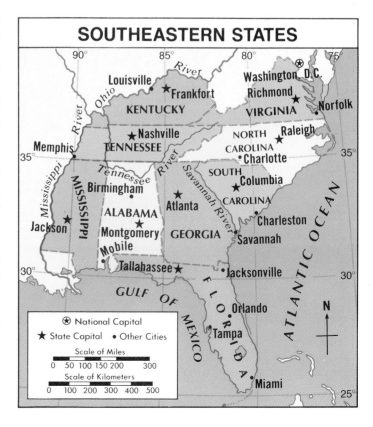

# LANDFORMS AND BODIES OF WATER

Unlike political boundaries, some symbols shown on maps are visible on Earth. Our planet has different shapes of land called **landforms**. The highest form of land on Earth is a **mountain**.

A single mountain, or its pointed top, may be called a **peak**. A low place, where it is easier to cross the mountains, is a **pass**. A group of mountains is a **mountain range**. A series of ranges makes up a **mountain system**. The land along the top of connected mountains is a **ridge**.

Some mountains are known as volcanoes. A **volcano** is built up by hot melted rock ejected from an opening in the earth. Many volcanoes are shaped like cones.

In high, cold mountains, glaciers may form. A **glacier** is a huge, slow-moving mass of ice that flows across the land.

Two other kinds of high land are hills and plateaus. A **hill** is not as high as a mountain. A steep-sided hill that is flat on top is called a

**mesa**. Hills near the bottom of a mountain are called **foothills**.

A **plateau** is a large area of high land that is flat on top. It is also called a **tableland**. A **piedmont** is a plateau region extending from foothills to a place at which the land drops. This point is called the **fall line**. Here, **waterfalls** form where a river drops to a lower level.

An area of low land between hills or mountains is a **valley**. A valley often has a river running through it. A **canyon** is a narrow valley with high, steep sides. The Grand Canyon in Arizona was carved by a river flowing over a plateau.

A **plain** is a large area of flat land. There are plains in the middle of North America and along the coasts. A **coast** is land bordering an ocean or sea. Coastal plains are lowlands. Swamps are found near the coast. **Swamps** are lowlands which are mostly covered with shallow water.

Along a coast, you will also find **peninsu-**

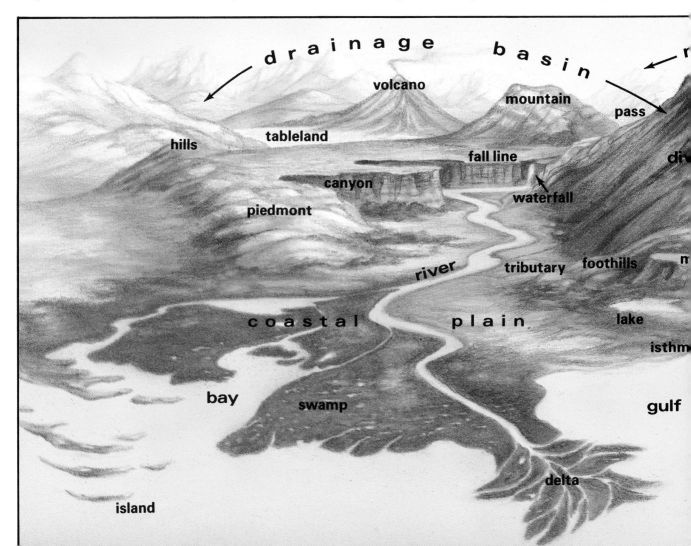

las, or "almost islands." Peninsulas are land surrounded by water on all sides but one. An **isthmus** is a narrow strip of land joining larger land areas. It may join a peninsula to the mainland. A **cape** is a point of land that projects out into an ocean or sea. You know that an **island** is a piece of land completely surrounded by water. A large group of islands is an **archipelago**.

Bodies of water are also shown on maps and in the picture below. A **river** is a large, natural stream that carries water. The **source** of a river, or place where it starts, is usually in the highlands. It may be a **lake**, a body of water completely surrounded by land. It may be a **spring** bubbling up out of the earth. Or it may be melting ice and snow from a glacier.

The **mouth of a river** is the place where it empties into a larger body of water. A river may drop rich soil at its mouth to form a low, triangular plain called a **delta**. A river or stream that flows into a larger river is a **tributary**. The land drained by a river and its tributaries is its **drainage basin**. A ridge separating drainage basins is a **divide**.

A **sea** is a large body of water smaller than an ocean. A **gulf** or **bay** is usually connected to an ocean or sea and is partly surrounded by land. An **inlet** is a small bay. A long, narrow inlet with high, steep banks is a **fjord**.

A passage of water connecting two larger bodies of water may be called a **strait** or **sound**. Usually a strait is very narrow. A sound often separates an island and the mainland.

**1.** Look at the drawing of landforms and bodies of water. Where would you build:
a. a road across the mountains?
b. a seaport city?
c. a bridge or tunnel? d. a railroad from mountains to coast? **2.** Where might you find a vacation resort?

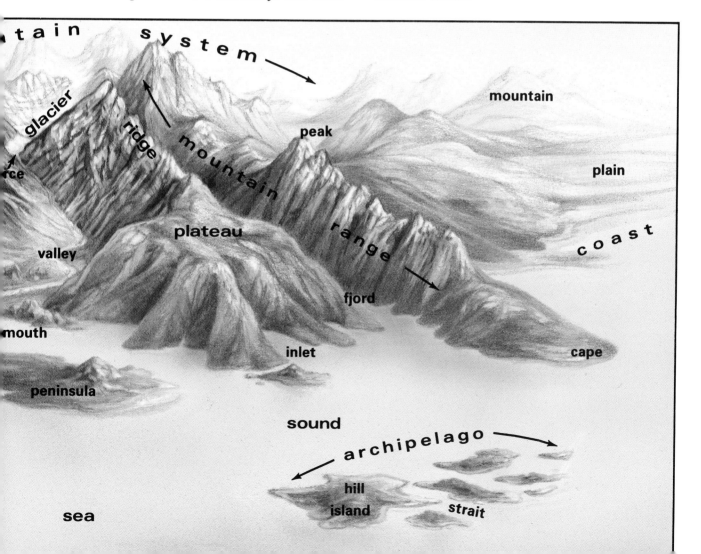

# PHYSICAL MAPS

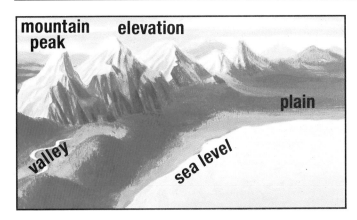

A **physical map** shows Earth's landforms and bodies of water. It is a way of picturing what the land looks like in different places. Earth has **highlands**, such as mountains and plateaus, and **lowlands**, such as plains and valleys. Symbols on a map can show how high or low the land is.

The height of land is its altitude or elevation. To measure land's **elevation**, you start at sea level, not ground level. **Sea level** is the height of the ocean where it meets the land along the coast.

Suppose you wanted to find the elevation of Cadillac Mountain on Mount Desert Island off the coast of Maine. You would measure straight up from sea level to a point even with the top of the mountain. The elevation of Cadillac Mountain is about 1,500 feet.

Next, suppose you want to measure the elevation of Pikes Peak in Colorado. That mountain is only 7,500 feet above ground level, but over 14,000 feet above sea level. You would need to know how high above sea level the ground at the bottom of the mountain is before you start to measure.

The most common way to show elevation on a physical map is with color. Different colors are used for different elevation ranges, from land below sea level to the highest mountains. Lowlands are usually shown as green. Highlands are usually orange, red or brown.

Look at the stairstep drawing and the physical map below. North America's coastal plains are between sea level and 500 feet in elevation. Inland are higher plains going up to 2,000 feet and 5,000 feet. The Great Plains region, a plateau in the middle of the continent, is as high as the Appalachian Mountains. The Rocky Mountains are much higher, with elevations ranging from 5,000 to over 14,000 feet. Is North America's highest land in the East or in the West?

As you can see, some plateaus are as high as some mountains. So you cannot tell these landforms apart on a color elevations map unless they are labeled.

## PHYSICAL MAP of NORTH AMERICA

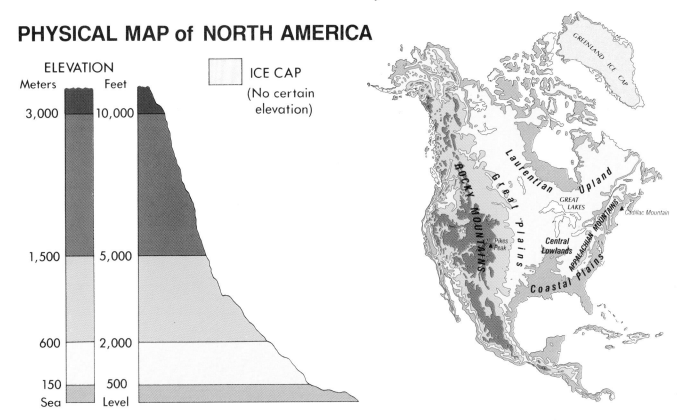

Another way a map can show elevation is with lines and shading. On such a map, mountains look wrinkled. They are shown in **relief**, seeming to stand out from the lower lands around them. On a globe with raised relief, you can feel mountain ridges with your fingers.

The map of California on the right uses lines, shading and colors to show different elevations. Find California's largest valley. Is it in the middle of the state or near a border? Are the highest mountains in the east or west?

A third way mapmakers show elevation is by using **contour lines**. These lines connect points of equal elevation. The elevations may be written on the lines. When contour lines are close together the land is very steep.

Look at the drawings below. Find the contour lines near the top of the mountain. Then look at the color key. What is the elevation of the land around the mountain peak?

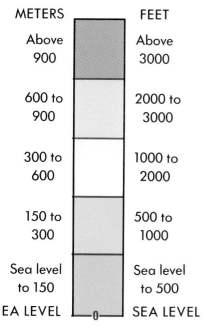

**1.** How can Pikes Peak have an elevation of 14,000 feet when it is only 7,500 feet above the ground?   **2.** How can you tell mountains and plateaus apart on a relief map? On a contour map?   **3.** Suppose you were planning a hike. How might a physical map help you?

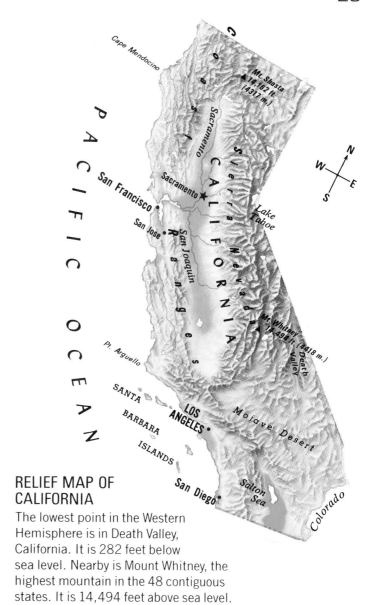

### RELIEF MAP OF CALIFORNIA

The lowest point in the Western Hemisphere is in Death Valley, California. It is 282 feet below sea level. Nearby is Mount Whitney, the highest mountain in the 48 contiguous states. It is 14,494 feet above sea level.

## CONTOUR MAP — Elevations shown in feet

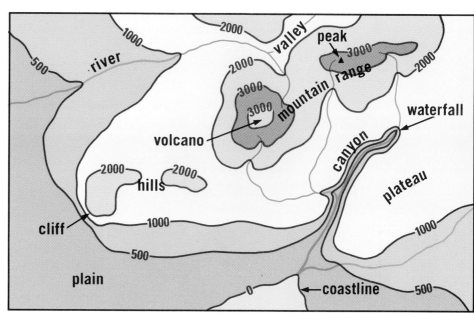

| METERS | | FEET |
|---|---|---|
| Above 900 | | Above 3000 |
| 600 to 900 | | 2000 to 3000 |
| 300 to 600 | | 1000 to 2000 |
| 150 to 300 | | 500 to 1000 |
| Sea level to 150 | | Sea level to 500 |
| EA LEVEL | 0 | SEA LEVEL |

# ROAD MAPS

A **road map** shows roads and what towns and cities they connect. It tells you something about what these roads are like. It may also help you figure out driving distance between places.

Look at the symbols in the road map key below. Different symbols show different kinds of highways. The largest roads are **limited access** highways. They are often called expressways or freeways. They have special entrances and exits so traffic lights are not needed. Vehicles can safely move faster on these roads.

In the United States, many limited access highways are linked together in the **Interstate Highway** system. They are numbered to make it

easier for drivers to know which road they are using.

Other highways also have numbers. They may be **Federal** routes connecting states. These highways are also called U.S. routes. **State** routes connect places within one state. Still other roads may be county or local routes.

Road maps use different shapes, or **shields**, to identify route numbers for each type of road. Notice the different shields used on the map of southern Arizona below. What different highways are shown?

To find the road distance between places we must use a different method than measuring

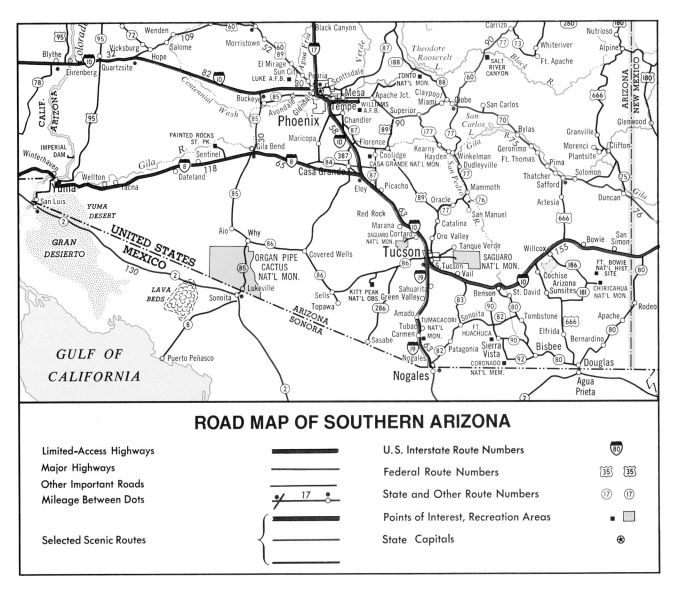

## ROAD MAP OF SOUTHERN ARIZONA

Limited-Access Highways

Major Highways

Other Important Roads

Mileage Between Dots — 17

Selected Scenic Routes

U.S. Interstate Route Numbers — 80

Federal Route Numbers — 35  35

State and Other Route Numbers — 17  17

Points of Interest, Recreation Areas — ■  ▢

State Capitals — ⊛

with a distance scale. Since roads bend and curve, a straight line distance doesn't tell us how far we must drive to get to a place.

The road maps on these pages use red numbers to show the mileage between red dots. Find I-8 south of Phoenix. What is the mileage from Gila Bend west to Yuma?

The map below is a closeup road map of Tampa and St. Petersburg, Florida. This is a map of a metropolitan area where many people live. It shows cities and their neighboring suburbs. Four of the larger cities are shown in yellow. Road maps often show city areas in this way.

92 south for three miles to Interstate 275. Follow I-275 west for two miles to State Route 60. Follow Route 60 west for 17 miles to Clearwater. What raised roadway takes you across Old Tampa Bay? What was your total mileage?

From Clearwater, what road would you take to reach Treasure Island? Why does this name appear on the map twice? When you get there, what museum could you visit nearby?

Congratulations! You have learned to navigate using a road map. You're now qualified to occupy the front passenger seat as map reader on your next car trip.

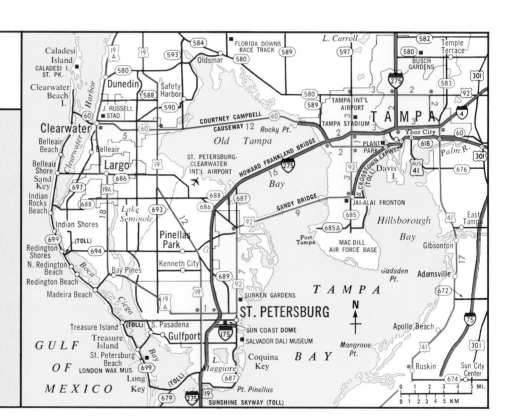

## ROAD MAP OF TAMPA BAY

Location and movement are two of geography's fundamental themes. Directions tell about relative location, or where one place is in relation to another. Latitude and longitude tell about absolute location, the fixed position of a place on our planet. Road maps show you ways to move from place to place. When people move, they carry their goods and ideas with them. They also see and learn new things. Thus, simply by traveling, people bring about change.

Let's learn to navigate using a road map.

Try tracing routes. What Interstate highway would you take from Busch Gardens in Tampa to the Sun Coast Dome in St. Petersburg? What bridge would you use?

What highway would you take from Tampa International Airport across the Gandy Bridge?

Start at Tampa Airport again. Take U.S. Route

**1.** If a local road ran for 30 miles between two towns, and an Interstate Highway was 32 miles between the same two towns, which would probably be the quickest way to get from one town to the other? Why? **2.** Using the U.S. political map on page 41, can you guess which states I-10 passes through on its way from Florida to California?

# DISTRIBUTION MAPS

Maps can help you find people and things as well as places. A **distribution map** shows how people or things are spread out over an area.

One familiar kind of distribution map shows natural resources or products. A **natural resource** is anything in nature that people can use. Some resources are living things, such as plants and animals. Others are nonliving things found in or on Earth, such as water and soil, coal and oil, gold and silver. People use resources for food, clothing, shelter, fuel and many other purposes.

Some resources are ready to use. Other resources are raw materials that are used to make finished goods. Look at the map of North America's leading products. Find two resources that are used as food. Find a resource that people use to make clothing.

 Suppose you were going to live in another country. Would you want to know what resources it had and where they were? Why would this be helpful?

## LEADING PRODUCTS

A distribution map can also show you where people live. Every 10 years the United States counts the people in each city, town and village. This is called a **census**. The facts found in a census may be shown on a distribution map.

Look at the **population map** of North America. It uses colors to show you which parts of the continent are crowded. Find the United States. Which part of our country is more crowded, the eastern half or the western half? Do more people live in the Northeast or the Northwest? Can you locate parts of North America where no one lives?

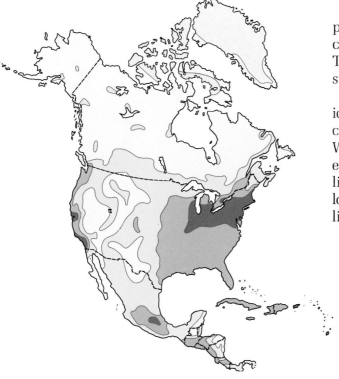

## POPULATION

| | |
|---|---|
| ▓ | **VERY CROWDED LANDS** |
| ▒ | **CROWDED LANDS** |
| □ | **LESS CROWDED LANDS** |
| □ | **ALMOST EMPTY LANDS** |
| ░ | **LANDS WHERE NO ONE LIVES** |

A very crowded, or densely populated, area has many people living close together. Would you expect to find many cities in such an area? Would you expect to find fewer cities in a less crowded, or sparsely populated, area? Why might people want to settle in or near a city?

A **vegetation map** is another kind of distribution map. **Vegetation** is plant life. Locate different regions on this vegetation map of North America.

Near the North Pole, the ground is always covered with thick ice. This cold **icecap** is an area where no plants grow. South of the icecap is the tundra and alpine region. Plants with deep roots cannot grow here. The **tundra** is a treeless plain where the soil beneath the surface stays frozen all year. In the spring and summer, moss and flowering plants appear. **Alpine** vegetation grows on high mountains. It is like the vegetation on the tundra. Wind and cold keep these plants from growing very tall. The **timberline** is the elevation above which trees cannot grow and only alpine plants are found.

Next comes the **forest** region, where there is enough rainfall for tall trees to grow. South of Canada's great forests are farmlands, grasslands and deserts. **Farmland** is flat, or rolling, with fertile soil and enough warmth and rainfall for crops to grow. A **grassland** region gets enough rain for grass, but not enough for tall trees. A **desert** is dry all year. Few plants can grow there.

Find your part of the country on the vegetation map. Then locate that color in the map key. In what vegetation area do you live?

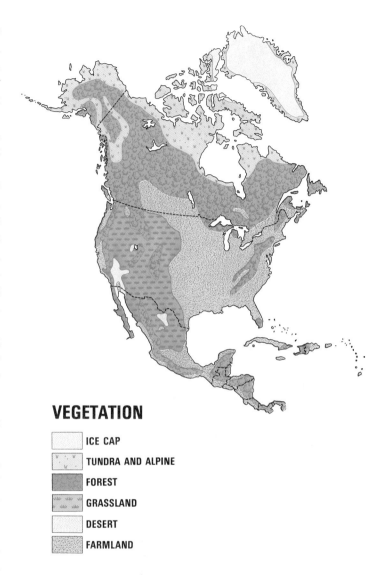

**VEGETATION**

- ICE CAP
- TUNDRA AND ALPINE
- FOREST
- GRASSLAND
- DESERT
- FARMLAND

Compare the vegetation map on this page and the population map on the facing page. In what vegetation area are most of the very crowded lands? Why do you think this is so?

**PAST & PRESENT** More than 200 years ago, in 1787, the founders of the United States drew up the Constitution. It is the basic law of the land. It says that every 10 years Congress must count the people. The more people a state has, the more representatives it can have in Congress.

The first United States census takers started work in 1790. They rode from place to place on horseback. In those days, there were fewer than 4 million Americans. By 1980 there were 235 million! The latest census was taken in 1990. When will the next census be?

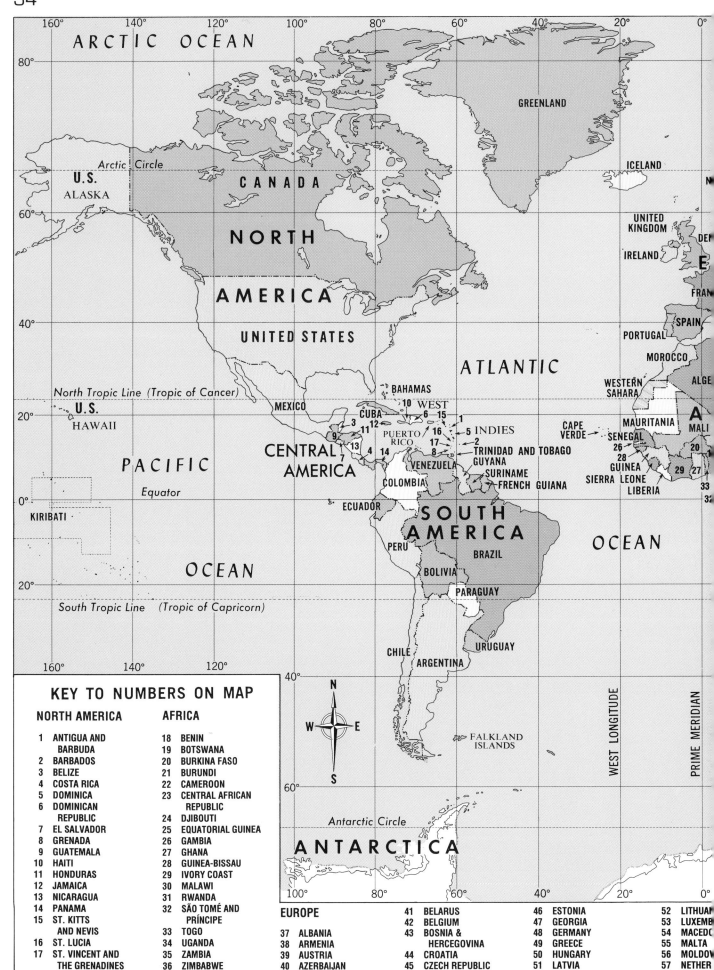

ARCTIC OCEAN

GREENLAND

ICELAND

U.S.
ALASKA

*Arctic Circle*

CANADA

NORTH

AMERICA

UNITED KINGDOM

IRELAND

*North Tropic Line (Tropic of Cancer)*

UNITED STATES

ATLANTIC

PORTUGAL

SPAIN

MOROCCO

WESTERN
SAHARA

MAURITANIA

U.S.
HAWAII

MEXICO

BAHAMAS

CUBA

10 WEST

6 15

1

5 INDIES

2

3

12

11

PUERTO
RICO

16

17

8

TRINIDAD AND TOBAGO

CAPE
VERDE

SENEGAL

MALI

20

26

28

GUINEA

29 27

PACIFIC

9

13

7

4 14

CENTRAL
AMERICA

VENEZUELA

GUYANA
SURINAME
FRENCH GUIANA

SIERRA LEONE
LIBERIA

33

*Equator*

COLOMBIA

ECUADOR

SOUTH
AMERICA

OCEAN

32

KIRIBATI

PERU

BRAZIL

OCEAN

BOLIVIA

*South Tropic Line   (Tropic of Capricorn)*

PARAGUAY

URUGUAY

CHILE

ARGENTINA

N

W        E

S

FALKLAND
ISLANDS

WEST LONGITUDE

PRIME MERIDIAN

*Antarctic Circle*

ANTARCTICA

## KEY TO NUMBERS ON MAP

### NORTH AMERICA

1 ANTIGUA AND
  BARBUDA
2 BARBADOS
3 BELIZE
4 COSTA RICA
5 DOMINICA
6 DOMINICAN
  REPUBLIC
7 EL SALVADOR
8 GRENADA
9 GUATEMALA
10 HAITI
11 HONDURAS
12 JAMAICA
13 NICARAGUA
14 PANAMA
15 ST. KITTS
  AND NEVIS
16 ST. LUCIA
17 ST. VINCENT AND
  THE GRENADINES

### AFRICA

18 BENIN
19 BOTSWANA
20 BURKINA FASO
21 BURUNDI
22 CAMEROON
23 CENTRAL AFRICAN
  REPUBLIC
24 DJIBOUTI
25 EQUATORIAL GUINEA
26 GAMBIA
27 GHANA
28 GUINEA-BISSAU
29 IVORY COAST
30 MALAWI
31 RWANDA
32 SÃO TOMÉ AND
  PRÍNCIPE
33 TOGO
34 UGANDA
35 ZAMBIA
36 ZIMBABWE

### EUROPE

37 ALBANIA
38 ARMENIA
39 AUSTRIA
40 AZERBAIJAN

41 BELARUS
42 BELGIUM
43 BOSNIA &
  HERCEGOVINA
44 CROATIA
45 CZECH REPUBLIC

46 ESTONIA
47 GEORGIA
48 GERMANY
49 GREECE
50 HUNGARY
51 LATVIA

52 LITHUAN
53 LUXEMB
54 MACEDO
55 MALTA
56 MOLDOV
57 NETHER

ARCTIC OCEAN

FINLAND

RUSSIA

46
51
52 41
59
58 56
62 1
54
49
BULGARIA 47
38 40
TURKEY 77
67 75
72 IRAQ IRAN
68 69
70 64 73
EGYPT SAUDI
ARABIA 78 OMAN
80
SUDAN 24
23
ETHIOPIA
31 34 SOMALIA
ZAIRE
21 KENYA
TANZANIA
30 COMOROS
35
36 MOZAMBIQUE MADAGASCAR
19 MAURITIUS
SWAZILAND
SOUTH LESOTHO
AFRICA

KAZAKHSTAN

79 A 71
76
63
PAKISTAN
NEPAL 65
INDIA

MONGOLIA

NORTH
KOREA
SOUTH
KOREA JAPAN
CHINA

BHUTAN
LAOS TAIWAN
BURMA
THAILAND 66 VIETNAM
SRI
LANKA BRUNEI
MALAYSIA
MALDIVES 74

SEYCHELLES

INDIAN

OCEAN

INDONESIA NEW GUINEA

PACIFIC

North Tropic Line (Tropic of Cancer)

PHILIPPINES

MICRONESIA OCEAN

MARSHALL
ISLANDS

Equator
NAURU
SOLOMON
ISLANDS
PAPUA
NEW
GUINEA
VANUATU

KIRIBATI

TUVALU
WESTERN SAMOA

FIJI
TONGA

AUSTRALIA

South Tropic Line
(Tropic of Capricorn)

NEW
ZEALAND

INTERNATIONAL DATE LINE

Arctic Circle

### THE WORLD
Modified Mercator Projection
EQUATORIAL SCALES
MILES
0    1000    2000

KILOMETERS
0    1000    2000

© Copyright HAMMOND INCORPORATED, Maplewood, N. J.

ANTARCTICA

Arctic Circle

Antarctic Circle

| 58 | ROMANIA | **ASIA** | | 67 | CYPRUS | 73 | QATAR | 78 | UNITED ARAB |
| 59 | SLOVAKIA | | | 68 | ISRAEL | 74 | SINGAPORE | | EMIRATES |
| 60 | SLOVENIA | 63 | AFGHANISTAN | 69 | JORDAN | 75 | SYRIA | 79 | UZBEKISTAN |
| 61 | SWITZERLAND | 64 | BAHRAIN | 70 | KUWAIT | 76 | TAJIKISTAN | 80 | YEMEN |
| 62 | YUGOSLAVIA | 65 | BANGLADESH | 71 | KYRGYZSTAN | 77 | TURKMENISTAN | | |
| | | 66 | CAMBODIA | 72 | LEBANON | | | | |

# NORTH AMERICA: OUR CONTINENT

North America is Earth's third-largest continent. Three of the world's four oceans border North America. Our continent joins South America at the narrow Isthmus of Panama. There, the Panama Canal connects the Atlantic and Pacific Oceans.

North America's size gives it a wide range of climates. Near the Arctic Ocean in the north, it is always cold. In the far south, it is always hot, except at high elevations. In between, a wide area of temperate climate has hot summers and cold winters.

Great seas, gulfs and bays cut into the mainland. Many peninsulas extend from the mainland. These features give North America the longest coastline of any continent. Many good harbors are found here.

North America has two major mountain systems. The rugged Rocky Mountains in the west and the Appalachian Mountains in the east rise on the edges of a vast central plain. Twin mountain ranges run down the Pacific coast.

East of these coast ranges is an arid plateau that stretches to the base of the Rocky Moun-

The United States has many big, busy cities with very tall buildings. This is a night view of the skyline of Houston, Texas.

tains. The Grand Canyon of the Colorado River is here. North America's largest deserts are also found here.

In Mexico, most of the people live on a high plateau between mountains. The climate here is cooler than on the coasts.

Look at the physical map on the next page. You can see the low coastal plains which border the Atlantic Ocean and the Gulf of Mexico. West of the Appalachian Mountains are interior plains drained by lengthy rivers.

Now look at the population map of North America. The most crowded region is in the eastern United States. This area is just south of the Great Lakes, the largest freshwater lakes in the world. People like to settle on flat, fertile land near good waterways.

## POPULATION

| | VERY CROWDED LANDS |
| --- | --- |
| | CROWDED LANDS |
| | LESS CROWDED LANDS |
| | ALMOST EMPTY LANDS |
| | LANDS WHERE NO ONE LIVES |

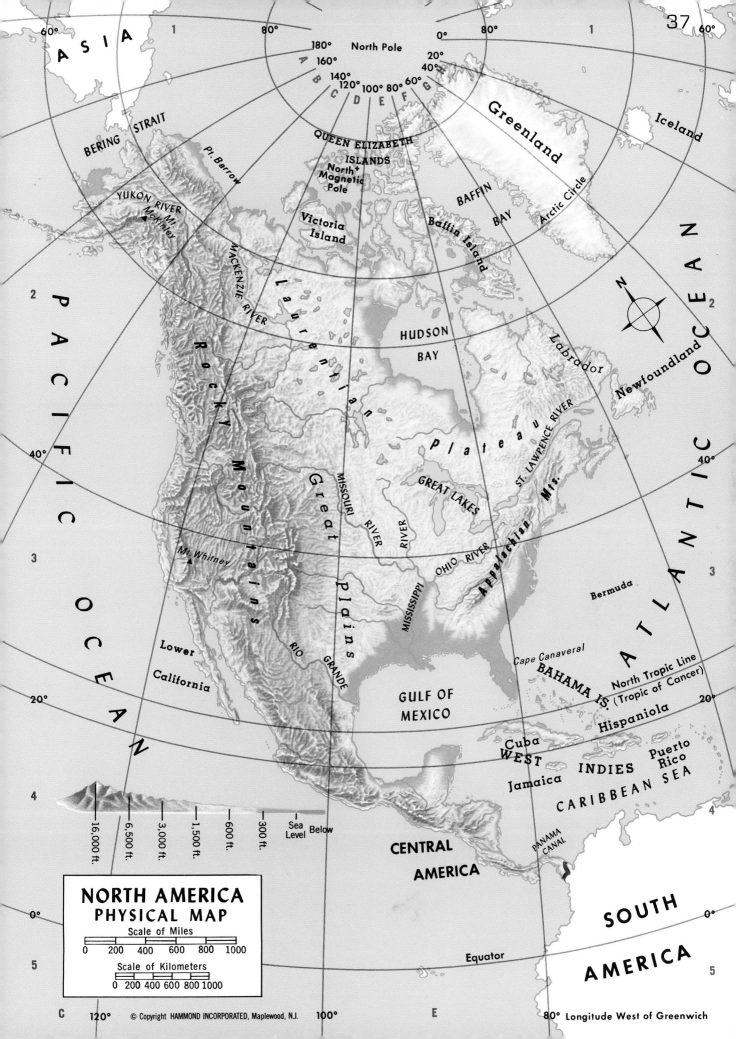

ASIA

60° 1 80° North Pole 0° Equator 80° 60°
180°
160°
A
B
140°
C
120° 100° 80° 60°
D E F G
20°
40°

Greenland

Iceland

BERING STRAIT

Pt. Barrow

QUEEN ELIZABETH
ISLANDS
North
Magnetic
Pole

BAFFIN

BAY

Arctic Circle

YUKON RIVER
Mt. McKinley

Victoria
Island

Baffin Island

MACKENZIE RIVER

Laurentian

HUDSON

BAY

Labrador

Newfoundland

N

2 2

P A C I F I C

R o c k y

M o u n t a i n s

P l a t e a u

GREAT LAKES

St. Lawrence River

40° 40°

Mt. Whitney

G r e a t

MISSOURI
RIVER

RIVER

OHIO RIVER

Appalachian Mts.

Bermuda

3 3

O C E A N

P l a i n s

RIO GRANDE

MISSISSIPPI

Cape Canaveral

BAHAMA IS.

North Tropic Line
(Tropic of Cancer)

Lower

California

GULF OF
MEXICO

Hispaniola

20° 20°

Cuba

WEST

INDIES

Puerto
Rico

Jamaica

CARIBBEAN SEA

4 4

16,000 ft.
6,500 ft.
3,000 ft.
1,500 ft.
600 ft.
300 ft.
Sea
Level
Below

CENTRAL

AMERICA

PANAMA
CANAL

SOUTH

0° 0°

NORTH AMERICA
PHYSICAL MAP

Scale of Miles

0 200 400 600 800 1000

Scale of Kilometers

0 200 400 600 800 1000

Equator

AMERICA

5 5

C 120° 100° E 80° Longitude West of Greenwich

© Copyright HAMMOND INCORPORATED, Maplewood, N.J.

ATLANTIC OCEAN

# NORTH AMERICA

Ten nations are located on the mainland of North America. Canada, the United States and Mexico take up most of the continent's land. Seven smaller countries lie between Mexico and South America. Find their names on the map on page 39. This area is called Central America. Still other nations are found on the islands of the Caribbean Sea.

The first Americans crossed from northeast Asia to Alaska thousands of years ago. These people were the ancestors of Native Americans, or American Indians. Much later, Europeans explored the continent and settled here. Today, Spanish, English and French are spoken and many of the customs and ideas they brought here are reflected around us.

*Mexicans gather at a famous church to celebrate a religious holiday. Mexican people enjoy many fiestas (festivals) during the year.*

## CONTINENT CLOSEUP

★ Mammoth Cave in Kentucky is Earth's largest, with 300 miles of passages.

★ A dozen island nations border the Caribbean Sea. Cuba is the largest. Many other islands are governed by nations outside the region.

★ Canada has the longest coastline of any country in the world.

★ At the Bering Strait, North America is only 2-1/2 miles from Asia.

## LEADING PRODUCTS

## VEGETATION

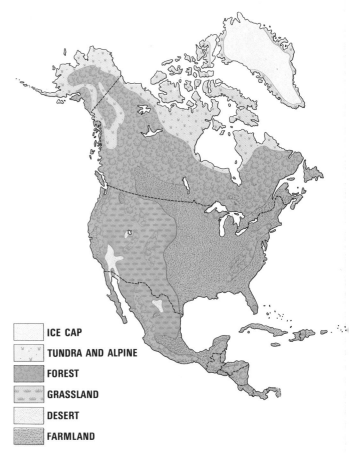

ICE CAP

TUNDRA AND ALPINE

FOREST

GRASSLAND

DESERT

FARMLAND

ASIA
RUSSIA

ARCTIC OCEAN

GREENLAND (Den.)

ICELAND

BERING STRAIT

UNITED STATES
ALASKA
YUKON R.
Pt. Barrow
Anchorage

QUEEN ELIZABETH ISLANDS

North Magnetic Pole

Victoria Island

MACKENZIE R.

BAFFIN BAY

Baffin Island

Arctic Circle

N

ATLANTIC OCEAN

Juneau

CANADA

HUDSON BAY

ST. LAWRENCE R.

PACIFIC OCEAN

Rocky Mountains

Edmonton

Seattle
Vancouver

Winnipeg

Montréal

San Francisco

Minneapolis

GREAT LAKES

Ottawa
Toronto
Mts.
Boston

Denver

MISSOURI R.

Detroit

New York

Los Angeles

UNITED STATES

Kansas City

Chicago

Cleveland

Philadelphia
Washington

St. Louis

OHIO R.

Appalachian

Bermuda (U.K.)

Lower California

Atlanta

MISSISSIPPI R.

Dallas

New Orleans

Cape Canaveral

BAHAMAS

North Tropic Line (Tropic of Cancer)

MEXICO

RIO GRANDE

Houston

GULF OF MEXICO

Miami

DOMINICAN REPUBLIC

Mexico City

CUBA

WEST

HAITI

PUERTO RICO (U.S.)

INDIES

JAMAICA

CARIBBEAN SEA

BELIZE

GUATEMALA
EL SALVADOR

HONDURAS

NICARAGUA

CENTRAL AMERICA

COSTA RICA

PANAMA CANAL

PANAMA

SOUTH AMERICA

Equator

## NORTH AMERICA
### POLITICAL MAP
Scale of Miles

0 200 400 600 800 1000

Scale of Kilometers

0 200 400 600 800 1000

© Copyright HAMMOND INCORPORATED, Maplewood, N.J.

80° Longitude West of Greenwich

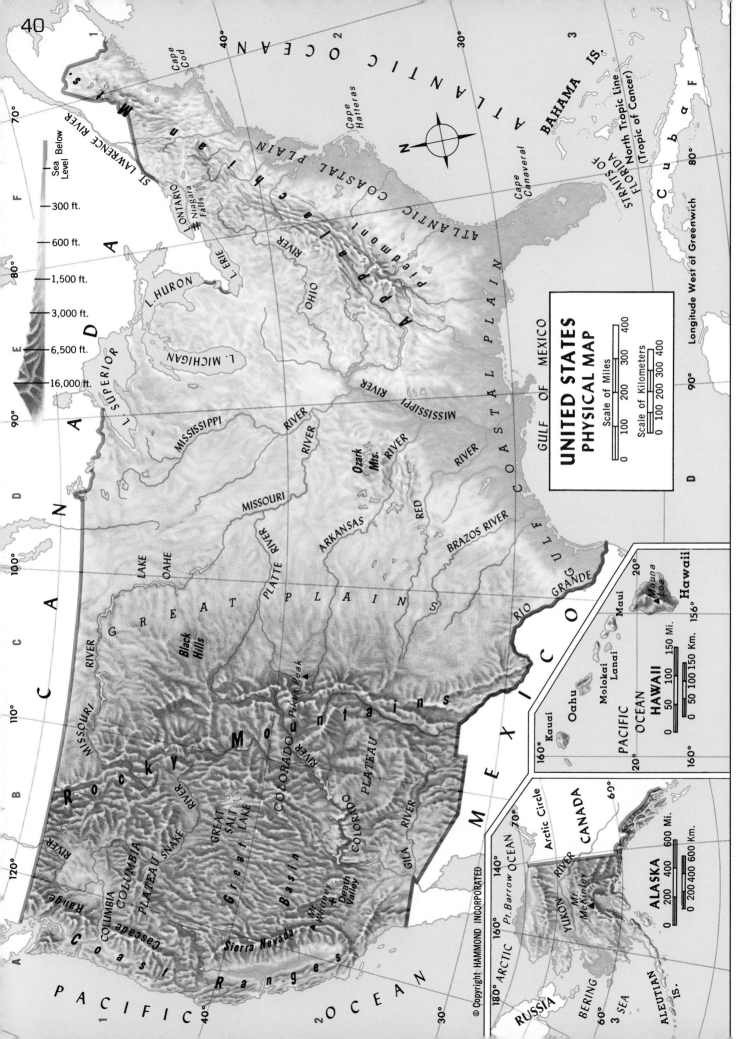

# UNITED STATES PHYSICAL MAP

Scale of Miles
0    100   200   300   400

Scale of Kilometers
0   100  200  300  400

© Copyright HAMMOND INCORPORATED

ATLANTIC OCEAN

PACIFIC OCEAN

CANADA

MEXICO

GULF OF MEXICO

Cape Cod
Cape Hatteras
Cape Canaveral
BAHAMA IS.
STRAITS OF FLORIDA
North Tropic Line (Tropic of Cancer)
Cuba
Longitude West of Greenwich

ST. LAWRENCE RIVER
L. ONTARIO
Niagara Falls
L. ERIE
L. HURON
L. MICHIGAN
L. SUPERIOR

Sea Level Below
300 ft.
600 ft.
1,500 ft.
3,000 ft.
6,500 ft.
16,000 ft.

Appalachian
Piedmont
ATLANTIC COASTAL PLAIN
COASTAL PLAIN

OHIO RIVER
MISSISSIPPI RIVER
MISSISSIPPI RIVER
MISSOURI RIVER
Ozark Mts.
ARKANSAS RIVER
RED RIVER
BRAZOS RIVER
RIO GRANDE
PLATTE RIVER
LAKE OAHE

GREAT PLAINS

Black Hills
Pikes Peak
Rocky Mountains
COLORADO RIVER
COLORADO PLATEAU
GILA RIVER
COLUMBIA PLATEAU
Snake RIVER
MISSOURI RIVER
COLUMBIA RIVER
Great Salt Lake
Great Basin
Death Valley
Whitney
Sierra Nevada
Cascade Range
Coast Ranges

## HAWAII

Kauai
Oahu
Molokai
Lanai
Maui
Hawaii
Mauna Loa
PACIFIC OCEAN

Scale
0   50   100   150 Mi.
0   50  100 150 Km.

## ALASKA

Pt. Barrow
ARCTIC OCEAN
Arctic Circle
CANADA
YUKON RIVER
Mt. McKinley
RUSSIA
BERING SEA
ALEUTIAN IS.

Scale
0   200   400   600 Mi.
0  200 400 600 Km.

### UNITED STATES POLITICAL MAP

Scale of Miles
0 100 200 300 400

Scale of Kilometers
0 100 200 300 400

© Copyright—HAMMOND INCORPORATED

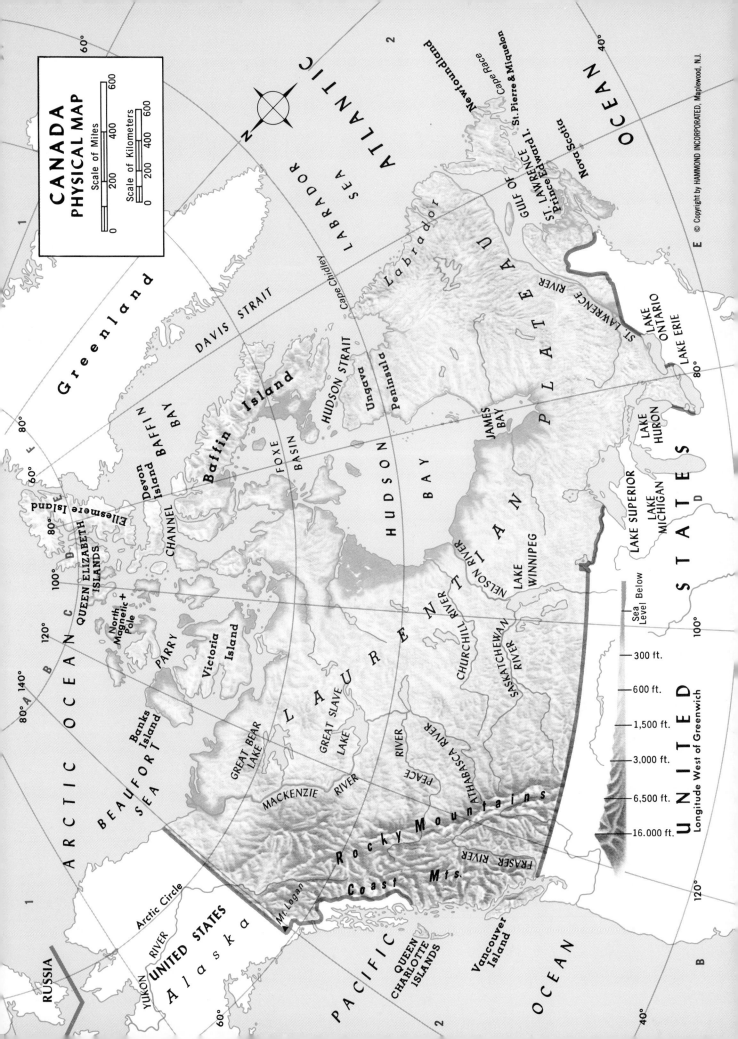

# CANADA
## PHYSICAL MAP

Scale of Miles
0    200    400    600

Scale of Kilometers
0    200    400    600

© Copyright by HAMMOND INCORPORATED, Maplewood, N.J.

ATLANTIC OCEAN

ATLANTIC

LABRADOR SEA

Greenland

DAVIS STRAIT

Newfoundland
Cape Race
St. Pierre & Miquelon
Prince Edward I.
GULF OF ST. LAWRENCE
Nova Scotia

BAFFIN BAY

Baffin Island

Cape Chidley

HUDSON STRAIT

Ungava Peninsula

Labrador

LAURENTIAN PLATEAU

ST. LAWRENCE RIVER

LAKE ONTARIO
LAKE ERIE

FOXE BASIN

HUDSON BAY

JAMES BAY

LAKE HURON

Devon Island

CHANNEL

Ellesmere Island

QUEEN ELIZABETH ISLANDS

North Magnetic Pole

PARRY

Victoria Island

LAKE SUPERIOR
LAKE MICHIGAN

NELSON RIVER

LAKE WINNIPEG

CHURCHILL RIVER

SASKATCHEWAN RIVER

U N I T E D   S T A T E S

ARCTIC OCEAN

Banks Island

BEAUFORT SEA

GREAT BEAR LAKE

GREAT SLAVE LAKE

RIVER

PEACE RIVER

ATHABASCA RIVER

Sea Level Below

—300 ft.
—600 ft.
—1,500 ft.
—3,000 ft.
—6,500 ft.
—16,000 ft.

Longitude West of Greenwich

MACKENZIE   RIVER

Rocky Mountains

FRASER RIVER

Coast Mts.

Mt. Logan

Arctic Circle

RUSSIA

YUKON RIVER

UNITED STATES
Alaska

QUEEN CHARLOTTE ISLANDS

Vancouver Island

PACIFIC OCEAN

60°   40°   80°   100°   120°

## CANADA POLITICAL MAP

Scale of Miles

0    200    400    600

Scale of Kilometers

0    200    400    600

ATLANTIC OCEAN

Newfoundland
St. John's
Cape Race
St. Pierre & Miquelon (Fr.)
Gander
GULF OF ST. LAWRENCE
PRINCE EDWARD ISLAND
Charlottetown
NEW BRUNSWICK
NOVA SCOTIA
Halifax
Fredericton
Labrador
LABRADOR SEA
Cape Chidley
NEWFOUNDLAND
Schefferville
Ungava Peninsula
QUÉBEC
R. ST. LAWRENCE
Québec
Montréal
Ottawa
TORONTO
LAKE ONTARIO
LAKE ERIE
Hamilton
Windsor

GREENLAND (Denmark)
DAVIS STRAIT
BAFFIN BAY
Devon Island
Baffin Island
HUDSON STRAIT
HUDSON BAY
JAMES BAY
ONTARIO
Timmins
Sudbury
LAKE HURON
LAKE SUPERIOR
LAKE MICHIGAN
Thunder Bay

Ellesmere Island
QUEEN ELIZABETH ISLANDS
CHANNEL
NORTHWEST TERRITORIES
North Magnetic Pole
PARRY
Victoria Island
GREAT BEAR LAKE
GREAT SLAVE LAKE
Yellowknife
Churchill
CHURCHILL R.
NELSON R.
MANITOBA
LAKE WINNIPEG
Winnipeg

ARCTIC OCEAN
BEAUFORT SEA
Banks Island
Inuvik
MACKENZIE R.
SASKATCHEWAN
SASKATCHEWAN
Saskatoon
Regina
ATHABASCA
PEACE R.
ALBERTA
Edmonton
Calgary
UNITED STATES

RUSSIA
UNITED STATES
ALASKA
YUKON TERRITORY
YUKON R.
Dawson
Whitehorse
Mt. Logan
Arctic Circle
Rocky Mountains
Coast Mts.
BRITISH COLUMBIA
FRASER R.
Prince Rupert
QUEEN CHARLOTTE ISLANDS
Vancouver Island
Vancouver
Victoria

PACIFIC OCEAN

Longitude West of Greenwich

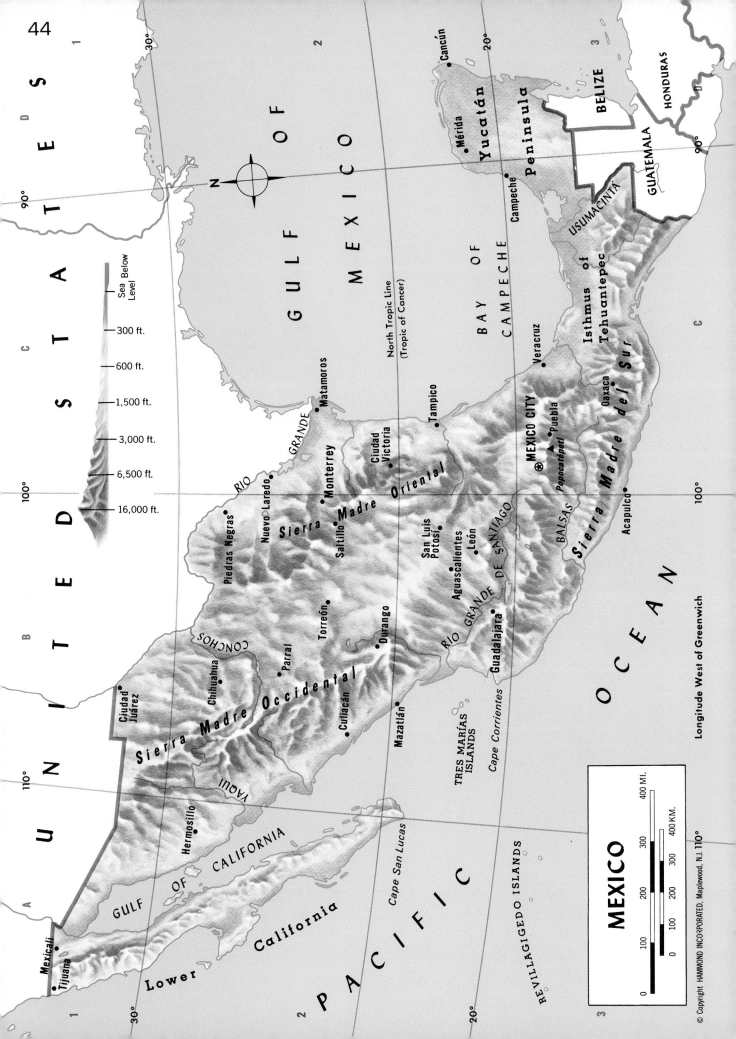

# MEXICO

UNITED STATES

GULF OF MEXICO

Sea Below Level
300 ft.
600 ft.
1,500 ft.
3,000 ft.
6,500 ft.
16,000 ft.

Cancún

Mérida

Yucatán Peninsula

BELIZE

HONDURAS

GUATEMALA

Campeche

BAY OF CAMPECHE

USUMACINTA

North Tropic Line
(Tropic of Cancer)

Veracruz

Isthmus of Tehuantepec

Matamoros

RIO GRANDE

Tampico

Ciudad Victoria

Monterrey

Sierra Madre Oriental

MEXICO CITY
Puebla
Popocatépetl

Oaxaca

Sierra Madre del Sur

Acapulco

Piedras Negras

Nuevo Laredo

Saltillo

San Luis Potosí

Aguascalientes

León

BALSAS

Ciudad Juárez

Chihuahua

Parral

Torreón

Durango

Cullacán

RIO GRANDE DE SANTIAGO

Guadalajara

CONCHOS

Sierra Madre Occidental

YAQUI

Hermosillo

Mazatlán

TRES MARÍAS ISLANDS

Cape Corrientes

Cape San Lucas

GULF OF CALIFORNIA

Lower California

Mexicali

Tijuana

REVILLAGIGEDO ISLANDS

PACIFIC OCEAN

Longitude West of Greenwich

400 MI.
300
200
100
0

400 KM.
300
200
100
0

© Copyright HAMMOND INCORPORATED, Maplewood, N.J. 110°

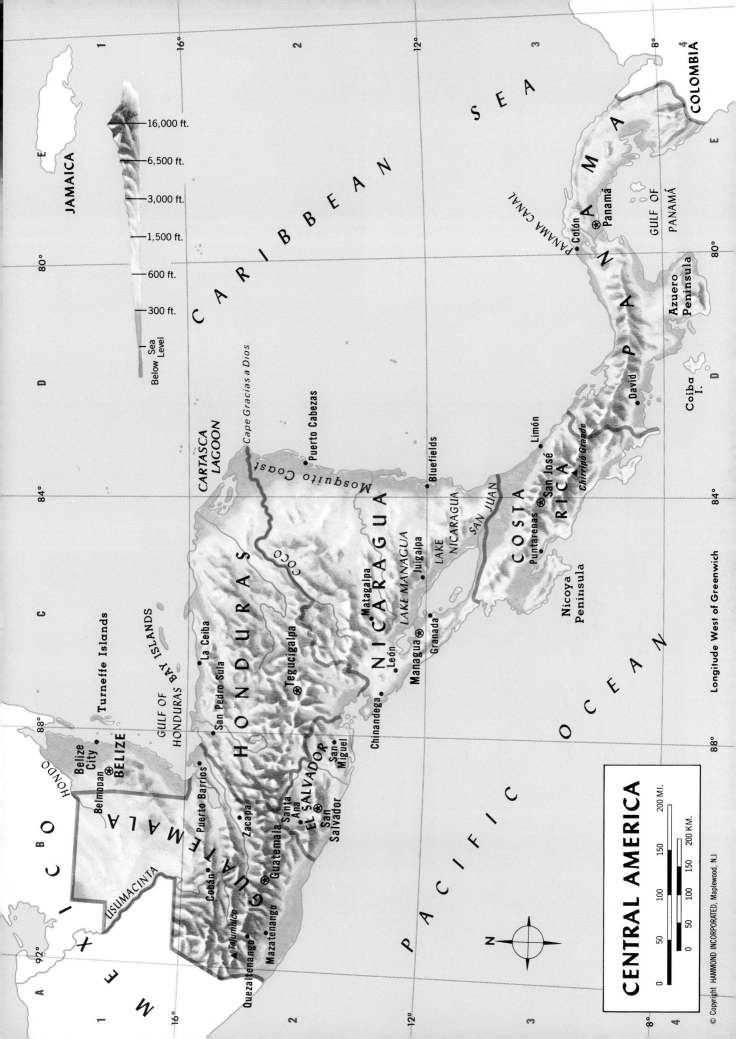

JAMAICA

E

C A R I B B E A N   S E A

1    16°              2         12°         3        8°
COLOMBIA

P A N A M A

PANAMA CANAL
Colón
Panamá
GULF OF PANAMÁ
Azuero Peninsula

80°

16,000 ft.
6,500 ft.
3,000 ft.
1,500 ft.
600 ft.
300 ft.
Sea Level
Below Level

David
Coiba I.

84°

Limón
San José
COSTA RICA
Chirripó Grande
Puntarenas
Nicoya Peninsula

CARTASCA LAGOON
Cape Gracias a Dios
Puerto Cabezas
Mosquito Coast

Bluefields

SAN JUAN
LAKE NICARAGUA
Juigalpa
Granada

N I C A R A G U A
COCO
Matagalpa
LAKE MANAGUA
Managua
León

Chinandega

88°

H O N D U R A S
La Ceiba
San Pedro Sula
Tegucigalpa

Turneffe Islands
GULF OF HONDURAS
BAY ISLANDS

BELIZE
Belize City
Belmopan
HONDO

Puerto Barrios
Zacapa
Santa Ana
EL SALVADOR
San Salvador
San Miguel

G U A T E M A L A
Cobán
Guatemala
Mazatenango
Quezaltenango
Tajumulco

M E X I C O
USUMACINTA

P A C I F I C   O C E A N

Longitude West of Greenwich

N

## CENTRAL AMERICA

200 MI.
0    50    100    150    200 KM.

© Copyright HAMMOND INCORPORATED, Maplewood, N.J.

# SOUTH AMERICA: OUR NEIGHBORING CONTINENT

South America is Earth's fourth-largest continent. In the north, it meets North America at the Isthmus of Panama. In the south, it is near the coldest continent, Antarctica. However, most of South America lies in the hot, tropic zone near the equator. It is bordered by the Atlantic and Pacific Oceans and the Caribbean Sea.

The equator crosses South America at the mouth of the Amazon River. The Amazon is the world's second-longest river and the one that carries the most water. In places, it is so wide a person cannot see across it.

The world's largest tropical rain forest, or selva, is found in the Amazon River Basin. This lowland region is always hot and wet. Trees grow so close together they form a tent-like roof, or canopy. Very little sunlight ever reaches the ground.

The Andes Mountains stretch like a backbone down the Pacific coast of South America. They are the longest and second-highest mountains on Earth. Many of the tallest peaks are volcanoes. Lake Titicaca, on a high plateau, is Earth's highest navigable lake.

There are many rich mineral deposits in South America. This open-pit copper mine is in Chile. Find out what copper is used for.

## POPULATION

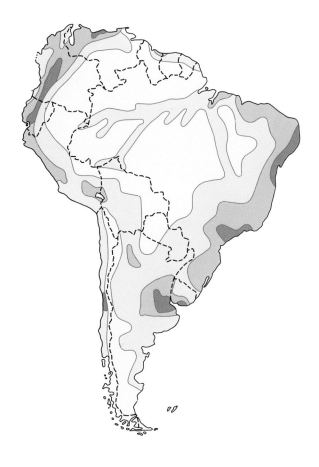

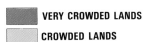 VERY CROWDED LANDS    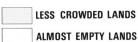 LESS CROWDED LANDS

CROWDED LANDS    ALMOST EMPTY LANDS

Large areas of South America have very few people. Much of the land is not easy to live on. In the north, the Llanos are hot, treeless plains. Dense forest covers the remote Guiana Highlands. In northern Chile, the Atacama Desert is one of the driest places on Earth. In the southeast, Patagonia is a dry, windswept region with poor soil.

Most South Americans live in just a few regions. The highlands of the northern Andes have a warm climate and long growing season. The Pampas are broad, fertile plains with a mild climate. Here, farmers grow wheat and corn, and ranchers raise sheep and cattle. The narrow coastal lowlands and nearby Brazilian Highlands have many people. Coffee and bananas are the main crops.

A  80°  CARIBBEAN  B  SEA  WEST  60°  C  40°  D

CENTRAL
AMERICA

*Punta Gallinas*

WEST
INDIES

ATLANTIC

OCEAN

1

LAKE
MARACAIBO

ORINOCO
RIVER

*Llanos*

*Angel
Falls*

*Guiana  Highlands*

1

Equator

0°
*RIO  NEGRO*
*AMAZON  RIVER*

*Cabo de
São Roque*

0°

*AMAZON  RIVER*

*S  e  l  v  a  s*

*RIO MADEIRA*

*RIO TAPAJÓS*

*Caatingas*

*RIO TOCANTINS*

*C  a  m  p  o  s*

*RIO SÃO FRANCISCO*

2

*A
n
d
e
s*

LAKE
TITICACA

*Mato Grosso
Plateau*

*B  r  a  z  i  l  i  a  n*

2

*M
o
u
n
t
a
i
n
s*

*Gran Chaco*

*H  i  g  h  l  a  n  d  s*

*PARANÁ*

P
A
C
I
F
I
C

20°

South Tropic Line
(Tropic of Capricorn)

20°

▲ *Dios del Salado*

*P
a
m
p
a
s*

RÍO

*RÍO URUGUAY*

3

▲ *Aconcagua*

*RÍO DE LA PLATA*

A
T
L
A
N
T
I
C

N

3

O
C
E
A
N

*Valdes Pen.*

O
C
E
A
N

40°

*P
a
t
a
g
o
n
i
a*

40°

FALKLAND
ISLANDS

### SOUTH AMERICA
### PHYSICAL MAP

Scale of Miles

| 0 | 200 | 400 | 600 | 800 |

Scale of Kilometers

| 0 | 200 | 400 | 600 | 800 |

STRAIT OF
MAGELLAN
**Tierra del
Fuego**

4

16,000 ft.  6,500 ft.  3,000 ft.  1,500 ft.  600 ft.  300 ft.  Sea Level  Below

4

*Cape Horn*

80°  B  60°  C Longitude West  40° of Greenwich  D  20°

# SOUTH AMERICA

South America has twelve nations and one state. Brazil is by far the largest country. Its people speak Portuguese. Spanish is the language in Venezuela, Colombia, Ecuador, Peru, Bolivia, Chile, Argentina, Paraguay and Uruguay. In Guyana, English is spoken. Dutch is the language of Suriname. French Guiana is a department, or state, of France.

The American Indians were the first people of South America. Over 450 years ago, they were conquered by Spanish soldiers from Europe. Today, most South Americans have European, African or American Indian heritage. Many are mestizos, part Indian and part European.

**LEADING PRODUCTS**

*Coffee berries are picked by hand when they turn bright red. Inside each berry are two coffee beans. The beans must be dried and roasted before using. Brazil and Colombia are the leading coffee-producing nations.*

## CONTINENT CLOSEUP

★ Brazil grows more oranges and coffee than any other nation on Earth.

★ The world's highest standard railroad is in Peru. It climbs the Andes to over three miles above sea level.

★ Large water mammals called manatees, or sea cows, live in the Amazon River, often growing to over 1,000 pounds.

★ La Paz, one of Bolivia's two capitals, is over two miles above sea level.

**VEGETATION**

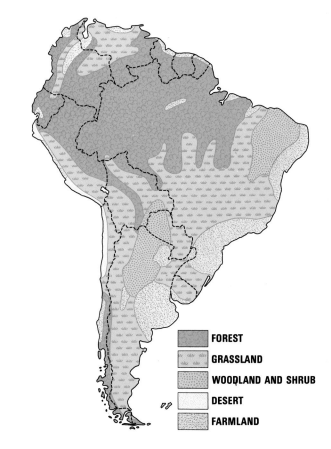

FOREST

GRASSLAND

WOODLAND AND SHRUB

DESERT

FARMLAND

49

# AFRICA: THE HOTTEST CONTINENT

Africa is the second-largest continent. It is bordered by the Atlantic and Indian Oceans and by the Mediterranean and Red Seas. In the northeast, Africa joins Asia at the Sinai Peninsula.

Africa is the hottest continent on Earth. The equator passes through the middle of the continent. Most of Africa lies in the tropic zone. Except in the highlands, the weather is hot all year. Once it was 136° in Libya, the highest temperature ever recorded on Earth.

Look at the physical map on the next page. The Sahara is the world's largest desert. It extends from the Atlantic Ocean to the Red Sea. At the equator, Africa is covered by a hot, wet rain forest. North and south of the equator, most of Africa is dry grassland or desert. Only the northwest and southern tips of the continent have mild climates.

Earth's longest river, the Nile, flows north from Lake Victoria to the Mediterranean Sea. At the mouth of the Nile is a wide, fertile delta. Good soil is also found along its banks over its entire course. In fact, the Nile River Valley is the world's largest oasis, a place in the desert with

## POPULATION

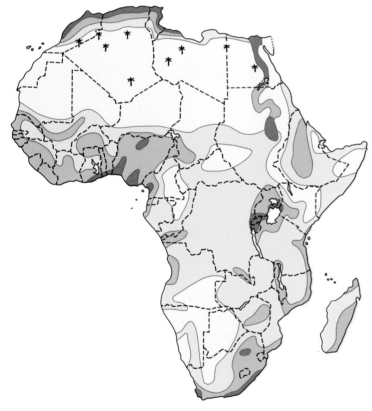

*Many wild animals live in Africa's dry grasslands. The giraffe is the tallest of all living animals. It can grow up to eighteen feet in height.*

water and fertile soil.

Look at the population map at the left. You can see that many people live along the Nile. The civilization of ancient Egypt centered around this great river.

Though Africa has long rivers, it lacks natural harbors along the coasts. Waterfalls and rapids prevent ships from sailing inland. Even so, most Africans live near rivers, lakes and coasts. The Niger and Congo Rivers are two other important waterways.

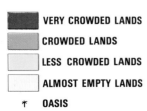

- ◼ VERY CROWDED LANDS
- ◼ CROWDED LANDS
- ◻ LESS CROWDED LANDS
- ◻ ALMOST EMPTY LANDS
- ⊤ OASIS

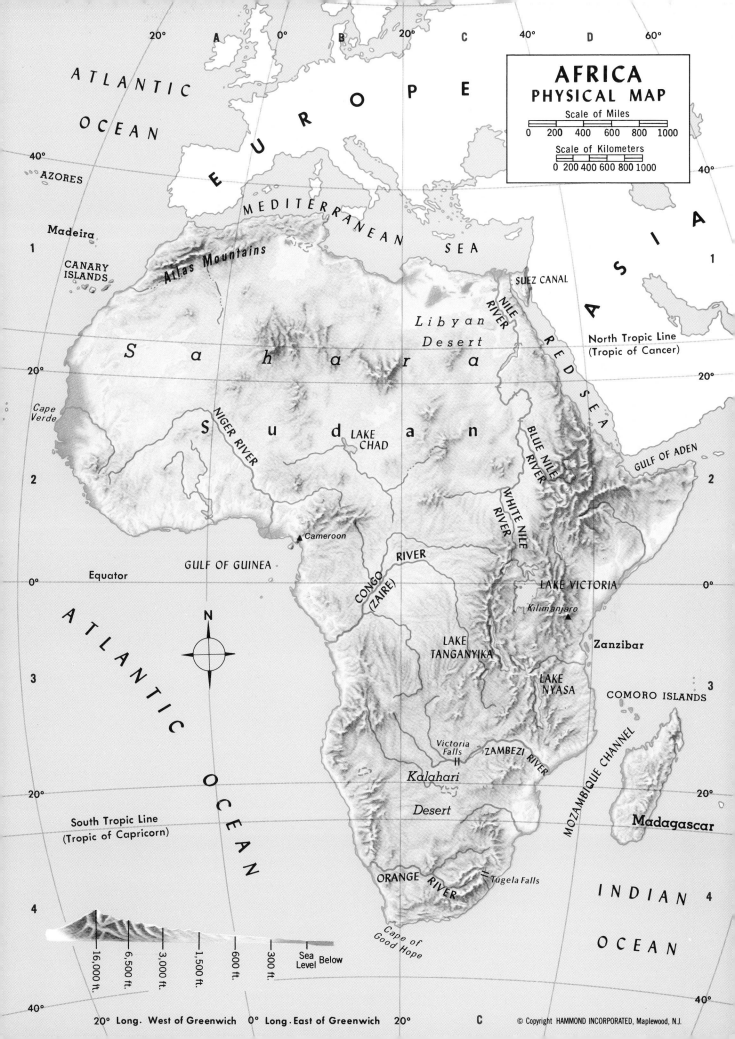

# AFRICA

Most of Africa is a low plateau. Africa's highlands are in the east along the Great Rift Valley. This region of large, deep lakes runs from the Red Sea to the Zambezi River. Animals such as giraffes, elephants, lions and zebras can be seen here.

There are more than fifty independent nations in Africa. Sudan is the largest and Nigeria has the most people. Africa's Arabs live in the north. Black Africans of many different ethnic groups live south of the Sahara. Each group has its own language, beliefs and customs. In fact, more than 800 languages are spoken in Africa.

Most Africans are farmers who live in small villages. Others herd cattle. Africans grow crops for their own use and for sale. Major exports include coffee, cocoa beans and cotton. Although little manufacturing is done in Africa, the continent has a wealth of resources, including gold, diamonds, copper and oil.

**LEADING PRODUCTS**

*The Sahara is the largest desert area in the world. Here an Arab rests his camel near the pyramids of Egypt. Why are camels so important for desert travel?*

## CONTINENT CLOSEUP

★ Ships sail inland over a thousand miles up the Congo, or Zaire, River.

★ The first human heart transplant took place in South Africa in 1967.

★ Millions of wild animals live on the Serengeti plain in Tanzania. They are protected from hunters.

★ Seventeen African nations became independent in 1960 alone.

**VEGETATION**

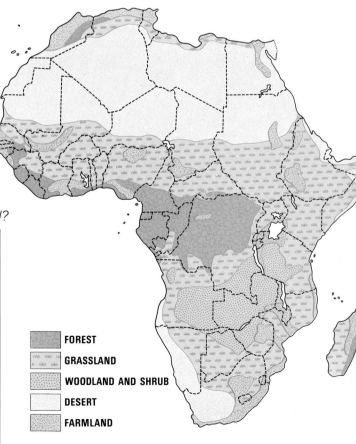

| | |
|---|---|
| ▨ | FOREST |
| ▨ | GRASSLAND |
| ▨ | WOODLAND AND SHRUB |
| ▨ | DESERT |
| ▨ | FARMLAND |

# AFRICA
## POLITICAL MAP

Scale of Miles
0  200  400  600  800  1000

Scale of Kilometers
0  200 400 600 800 1000

ATLANTIC

OCEAN

EUROPE

ASIA

AZORES
(Port.)

Madeira
(Port.)

CANARY
ISLANDS
(Sp.)

WESTERN

SAHARA

CAPE
VERDE

MEDITERRANEAN          SEA

Casablanca   Rabat      Algiers      Tunis
MOROCCO                              TUNISIA
         Atlas Mountains              Tripoli
                     Adrar        Al' Aziziyah    Benghazi

Alexandria
                                                  Cairo   SUEZ CANAL

ALGERIA          LIBYA          EGYPT

                                                  North Tropic Line
                                                  (Tropic of Cancer)

S   a   h   a   r   a

MAURITANIA                                NILE
  Nouakchott                                    Wadi
                    NIGER      CHAD              Halfa

Dakar                                     Khartoum
GAMBIA    Bamako                                              DJIBOUTI
SENEGAL                 NIGER      LAKE         SUDAN          GULF OF ADEN
GUINEA                             CHAD
BISSAU    GUINEA  BURKINA        N'Djamena                    Addis
2  Conakry        FASO   NIGERIA                     BLUE     Ababa
SIERRA LEONE       GHANA  BENIN                       NILE    ETHIOPIA
          IVORY    TOGO  Ibadan          CENTRAL
Monrovia  COAST          Lagos          AFRICAN REPUBLIC  WHITE NILE R.
LIBERIA   Abidjan Accra        CAMEROON  Bangui
          EQUATORIAL GUINEA   Yaounde              KENYA  SOMALIA
          GULF OF GUINEA                CONGO R. Kisangani
          SÃO TOMÉ & PRÍNCIPE                    UGANDA
Equator                         GABON           RWANDA  LAKE VICTORIA  Mogadishu
                                     CONGO  ZAIRE        Nairobi
                        Brazzaville              BURUNDI
                   CABINDA  Kinshasa   LAKE      TANZANIA  Zanzibar
                   (Ang.)            TANGANYIKA            Dar es Salaam
                                                 LAKE
                        Luanda                   NYASA    COMOROS

ATLANTIC                ANGOLA                   MALAWI
                                     ZAMBIA
                                     Lusaka  ZAMBEZI R.
OCEAN                                        Harare  MOZAMBIQUE  MADAGASCAR
                              NAMIBIA        ZIMBABWE           Antananarivo
South Tropic Line             Windhoek
(Tropic of Capricorn)                   BOTSWANA
                                     Gaborone  Pretoria
                                     Johannesburg  SOUTH AFRICA  Maputo
                                             ORANGE        SWAZILAND
                                             R.    Durban
                                     SOUTH AFRICA  LESOTHO
                        Cape Town                              INDIAN
                        Cape of Good Hope

                                                              OCEAN

© Copyright HAMMOND INCORPORATED, Maplewood, N.J.

20° Long. West of Greenwich   0° Long East of Greenwich   20°

54

# EUROPE: THE MOST CROWDED CONTINENT

Europe is the second-smallest continent. It stretches north to the cold Arctic Ocean and south to the warm Mediterranean Sea. The Atlantic Ocean borders Europe on the west. On the east, Europe meets Asia at the Ural Mountains and Caspian Sea. Since Europe and Asia are part of the same great expanse of land, some people think of them as one gigantic continent, **Eurasia.**

Europe may be thought of as a huge peninsula of Eurasia. It is broken into many smaller peninsulas. Look at the physical map on the next page.

## POPULATION

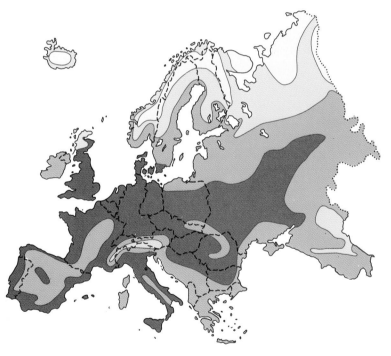

| | |
|---|---|
| ■ VERY CROWDED LANDS | ▫ LESS CROWDED LANDS |
| ▨ CROWDED LANDS | □ ALMOST EMPTY LANDS |

Find the Scandinavian Peninsula in the north and the Iberian and Balkan Peninsulas in the south.

On three sides, Europe's land is cut by seas, gulfs and bays. Most of Europe is close to a seacoast. Inland, great rivers, such as the Volga, Danube and Rhine, provide waterways. It is not surprising that Europeans became sailors and explorers. During the Age of Exploration, many European nations spread their languages and culture to the Americas.

Many of the continent's countries are isolated

*Europe is a small continent with a large population. Berlin, in Germany, is one of its large cities. How can you tell that it is a big city?*

by rugged mountains. The Alps run from southern France across the center of Europe to Yugoslavia. They separate Italy from its neighbors. The Pyrenees form a natural border between Spain and France. The Balkans and Carpathians also separate many small nations. Compare the physical and political maps of Europe to see which ones.

Most of Europe has a mild climate, even though it lies closer to the North Pole than to the equator. Warm breezes reach as far north as Norway. These winds are heated by the Gulf Stream, a warm current of the Atlantic Ocean.

Europe is the most crowded continent. Look at the population map at the right. Notice the very

(continued on page 56)

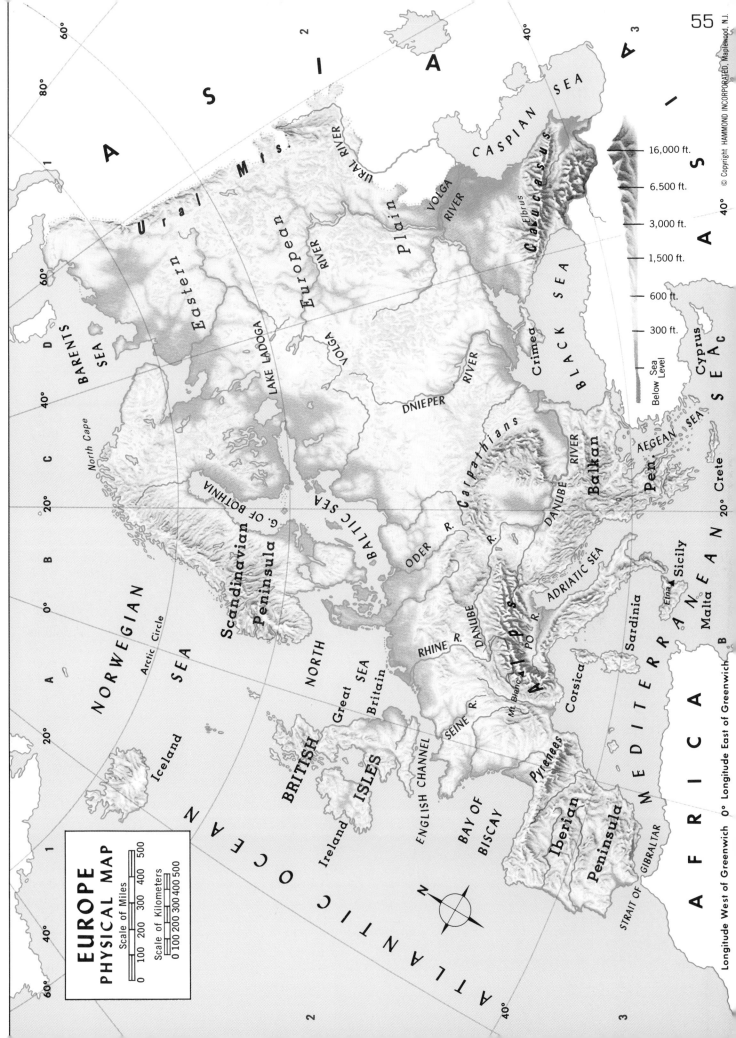

EUROPE
PHYSICAL MAP

Scale of Miles
0   100  200  300  400  500

Scale of Kilometers
0  100 200 300 400 500

16,000 ft.
6,500 ft.
3,000 ft.
1,500 ft.
600 ft.
300 ft.
Below Sea Level

A S I A

CASPIAN SEA

Caucasus

Elbrus

BLACK SEA

Crimea

AEGEAN SEA

Cyprus

SEA

Crete

MEDITERRANEAN SEA

Malta

Sicily

Etna

Sardinia

Corsica

ADRIATIC SEA

Balkan Pen.

Carpathians

DANUBE RIVER

DNIEPER RIVER

VOLGA RIVER

URAL RIVER

Eastern European Plain

Ural Mts.

VOLGA RIVER

ODER R.

BALTIC SEA

LAKE LADOGA

G. OF BOTHNIA

Scandinavian Peninsula

BARENTS SEA

North Cape

Arctic Circle

NORWEGIAN SEA

Iceland

ATLANTIC OCEAN

BRITISH ISLES

Ireland

Great Britain

NORTH SEA

ENGLISH CHANNEL

BAY OF BISCAY

Iberian Peninsula

Pyrenees

STRAIT OF GIBRALTAR

AFRICA

SEINE R.

RHINE R.

ALPS

Mt. Blanc

PO R.

DANUBE R.

N

AFRICA

© Copyright HAMMOND INCORPORATED, Maplewood, N.J.

Longitude West of Greenwich    0°  Longitude East of Greenwich

crowded lands that extend across the middle of the continent. Much of this strip is the fertile European Plain, a low region of excellent farmland. The leading products map shows that potatoes, sugar beets and grain crops are grown here.

Iron ore and coal are also plentiful. Together, they are used to make steel. Europe is very highly developed, with manufacturing centers throughout. In fact, this is where the Industrial Revolution began!

*Northern Europe has little good farmland. But its forests are an important resource. These logs are being towed to a sawmill Lumber, wood pulp, and paper are important products.*

Europe has over forty nations. Russia is the largest country in the world. It extends from Europe across Asia to the Pacific Ocean. Tiny Vatican City, the smallest nation, is the size of a few city blocks.

## CONTINENT CLOSEUP

★ Millions of people in the Netherlands live on land taken from the sea.

★ Poland is the world's second largest grower of potatoes. Over half of the world's olives come from Spain and Italy.

★ London had the first subway, in 1863, but Moscow's is the busiest, carrying over six million people a day.

★ Switzerland, surrounded by the Alps, has not been at war since 1515.

## LEADING PRODUCTS

## VEGETATION

| | |
|---|---|
| TUNDRA AND ALPINE | |
| FOREST | |
| GRASSLAND | |
| DESERT | |
| FARMLAND | |

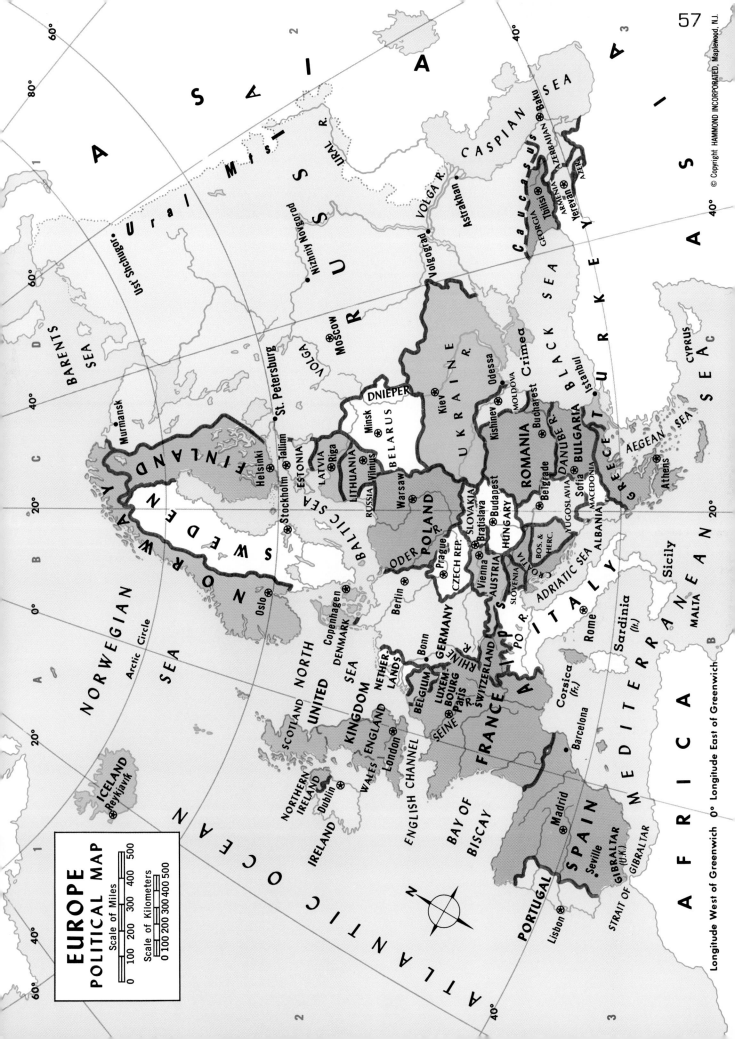

# ASIA: THE LARGEST CONTINENT

Asia ranks first in the world in many ways. It has more land and more people than any other continent. Earth's highest mountains, lowest land and deepest lake are here. Most of the largest nation, Russia, is in Asia. The two nations with the most people, China and India, are here.

Asia extends from frozen wastes at the Arctic Ocean to blistering deserts in the central and southwestern regions. Much of the continent's land cannot support more than a few people because of harsh climate.

Asia's coasts are carved into peninsulas. In the southwest, the Arabian Peninsula is the largest on Earth. Most of India is a peninsula, as is Indochina in the southeast.

Hundreds of islands, some small, some very large, form a chain at the edge of the Pacific Ocean, from the far north to south of the equator. Japan, the Philippines and Indonesia are among the nations that are found on these islands. Other smaller islands are also found in the Indian Ocean.

The Himalayas, between China and India, are the world's highest mountain system. Here is

## POPULATION

*Tokyo, Japan's capital, is the world's second largest city. It has tall buildings and busy streets. It has helped Japan become an industrial giant.*

Mount Everest, highest point on Earth. North of these mountains is Tibet, the largest and highest plateau on Earth.

Asia can be divided into six land regions. **Southwest Asia** extends from the Black Sea to the Arabian Sea. It is an area of large deserts and rich supplies of oil. India lies in **South Asia,** while Japan and China are in **East Asia.** These two regions are crossed by great rivers, have fertile farmland and mild climates. They are among the most densely populated places on Earth.

**Southeast Asia** includes the Indochina Peninsula and the islands nearby. This region is covered by tropical rain forests. It has a hot climate year round. In contrast, **North Asia** includes the plain of Siberia, the coldest inhabited area on Earth. **Central Asia** includes Mongolia and western China. Little rain falls in this area of high mountains, plateaus and deserts.

■ **VERY CROWDED LANDS**      ☐ **LESS CROWDED LANDS**
■ **CROWDED LANDS**           ☐ **ALMOST EMPTY LANDS**

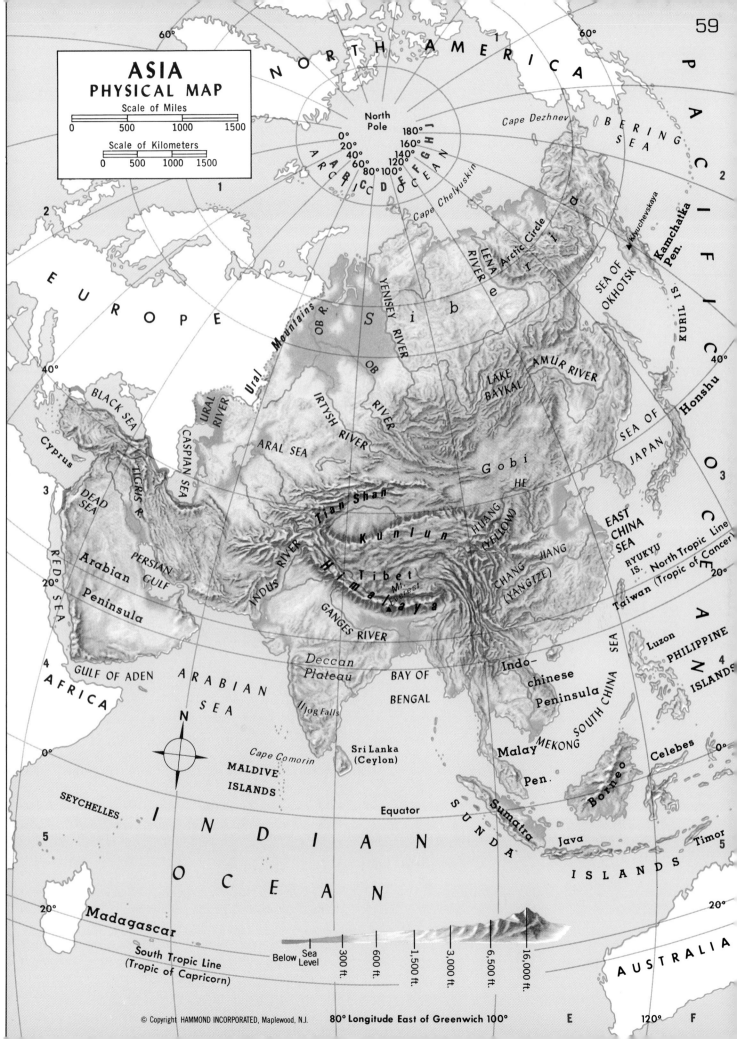

# ASIA
## PHYSICAL MAP

Scale of Miles

0   500   1000   1500

Scale of Kilometers

0   500   1000   1500

NORTH AMERICA

PACIFIC

North Pole

Cape Dezhnev

BERING SEA

ARCTIC OCEAN

Cape Chelyuskin

0° 20° 40° 60° 80° 100° 120° 140° 160° 180°

A B C D E F G H I J

Kamchatka Pen.

Klyuchevskaya

Siberia

Arctic Circle

LENA RIVER

YENISEY RIVER

SEA OF OKHOTSK

KURIL IS.

EUROPE

Ural Mountains

OB R.

OB RIVER

IRTYSH RIVER

LAKE BAYKAL

AMUR RIVER

Honshu

SEA OF JAPAN

BLACK SEA

URAL RIVER

ARAL SEA

CASPIAN SEA

Cyprus

Gobi

HE

PACIFIC OCEAN

DEAD SEA

TIGRIS R.

Tian Shan

Kunlun

HUANG (YELLOW)

JIANG

EAST CHINA SEA

RYUKYU IS.

North Tropic Line

(Tropic of Cancer)

RED SEA

Arabian

PERSIAN GULF

INDUS RIVER

Himalaya

Tibet

Mt. Everest

CHANG (YANGTZE)

Taiwan

Peninsula

GANGES RIVER

Deccan Plateau

BAY OF BENGAL

Indo-chinese

Luzon

PHILIPPINE ISLANDS

GULF OF ADEN

ARABIAN SEA

Jog Falls

Peninsula

Malay

MEKONG

SOUTH CHINA SEA

AFRICA

N

Cape Comorin

Sri Lanka (Ceylon)

MALDIVE ISLANDS

Pen.

Celebes

Borneo

SEYCHELLES

Equator

Sumatra

Java

Timor

INDIAN

SUNDA

ISLANDS

OCEAN

Madagascar

Below Sea Level  300 ft.  600 ft.  1,500 ft.  3,000 ft.  6,500 ft.  16,000 ft.

South Tropic Line
(Tropic of Capricorn)

AUSTRALIA

80° Longitude East of Greenwich 100°

120°

# ASIA

Asia has long been famous for its spices, tea and cotton. Rice and wheat are the most important food crops. Russia, China, Japan and South Korea manufacture many goods. Asia has many large, crowded cities such as Tokyo, Shanghai, Calcutta, and Seoul. Even so, most Asians still grow their own food and live in small, rural villages.

The world's earliest civilizations arose in Asia. All of the world's major religions began here. From Israel to India, from Saudi Arabia to Japan, Asians are as varied as their vast continent.

## LEADING PRODUCTS

*Some areas of Asia have fertile soils. In these places, farming is very important. This farmer is growing rice—Asia's chief food crop. Most farms are small. Most work is done by hand.*

## CONTINENT CLOSEUP

★ The Great Wall of China is more than 4,000 miles long.

★ Lake Baykal, in Russia, is over a mile deep in many parts.

★ Mount Everest, the world's highest peak, was first climbed in 1953 by Sir Edmund Hillary and Tenzing Norgay.

★ Over half the world's known oil reserves are found in Southwest Asia.

## VEGETATION

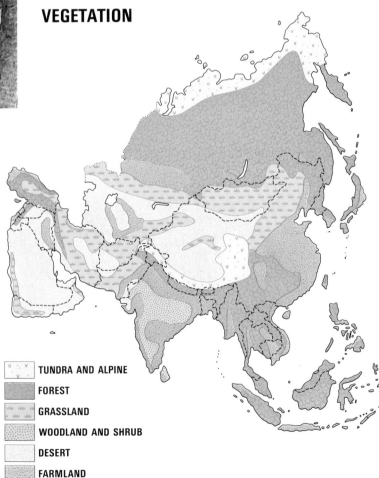

- TUNDRA AND ALPINE
- FOREST
- GRASSLAND
- WOODLAND AND SHRUB
- DESERT
- FARMLAND

## ASIA
### POLITICAL MAP
Scale of Miles

| | | | |
|---|---|---|---|
| 0 | 500 | 1000 | 1500 |

Scale of Kilometers

| | | | |
|---|---|---|---|
| 0 | 500 | 1000 | 1500 |

NORTH AMERICA

PACIFIC

North Pole

BERING SEA

Cape Dezhnev

Cape Chelyuskin

Kamchatka Pen.

KURIL IS.

ARCTIC OCEAN

Arctic Circle

LENA R.

Verhoyansk

SEA OF OKHOTSK

EUROPE

RUSSIA

Moscow

Sverdlovsk

OB R.

YENISEY

Chelyabinsk

Omsk

Novosibirsk

IRTYSH R.

OB R.

Irkutsk

LAKE BAYKAL

AMUR R.

Vladivostok

SEA OF JAPAN

Honshu

Tokyo

KAZAKHSTAN

ARAL SEA

CASPIAN SEA

URAL R.

Ulaanbaatar

MONGOLIA

Gobi

Shenyang

NORTH KOREA

Seoul

SOUTH KOREA

Osaka

JAPAN

BLACK SEA

TURKEY

Ankara

CYPRUS

LEBANON

SYRIA

ISRAEL

JORDAN

IRAQ

Baghdad

Tehran

IRAN

Abadan

KUWAIT

Tashkent

UZBEKISTAN

Alma-Ata

KYRGYZSTAN

TURKMENISTAN

TAJIKISTAN

AFGHANISTAN

Islamabad

Ürümqi

HUANG HE

Beijing

Tianjin

Lanzhou

CHINA

CHANG JIANG

Shanghai

Wuhan

Chongqing

RYUKYU IS.

North Tropic Line
(Tropic of Cancer)

SAUDI

Riyadh

Mecca

BAHRAIN

QATAR

UNITED ARAB EMIRATES

ARABIA

OMAN

San'a

YEMEN

Aden

GULF OF ADEN

RED SEA

AFRICA

Lahore

PAKISTAN

Karachi

New Delhi

Himalaya

NEPAL

INDUS R.

GANGES R.

BHUTAN

BANGLADESH

Cherrapunji

INDIA

Calcutta

BURMA

Hanoi

LAOS

TAIWAN

Guangzhou

HONG KONG
(U.K.)

Manila

PHILIPPINES

Bombay

Hyderabad

BAY OF BENGAL

Rangoon

THAILAND

Bangkok

VIETNAM

Ho Chi Minh City

CAMBODIA

SOUTH CHINA SEA

ARABIAN SEA

Madras

SRI LANKA

Cape Comorin

Colombo

MALDIVES

N

MEKONG

Malay Pen.

MALAYSIA

BRUNEI

Celebes

Equator

SEYCHELLES

Kuala Lumpur

SINGAPORE

Borneo

INDONESIA

Sumatra

SUNDA

Java

Surabaya

Timor

Jakarta

ISLANDS

INDIAN OCEAN

Madagascar

MAURITIUS

AUSTRALIA

South Tropic Line
(Tropic of Capricorn)

80° Longitude East of Greenwich 100°

# AUSTRALIA: THE SMALLEST CONTINENT

Australia is Earth's smallest continent. It lies southeast of Asia, between the Indian and Pacific Oceans. Australia, like an island, is completely surrounded by water. But Australia is over three times larger than the world's largest island, Greenland.

All of Australia is south of the equator. In fact, the name comes from the Latin word for "south". Many people refer to Australia as "the land down under", because it is at the "bottom" of the globe. Seasons are the opposite of those in the Northern Hemisphere. Winter begins in June and summer starts in December.

Australia's climate is warm and dry. Mild winters bring snow only to the highest mountains. These are found in the east. The Great Dividing Range runs the length of the continent. West of this range are the Central Lowlands. Little rain falls here and lakes often dry up completely. The Western Plateau extends to the Indian Ocean. It is flat and dry, either desert or arid grassland. Few people live west of the Great Dividing Range, except for some farmlands along the coasts.

*Sydney is a port on Australia's southeast coast. Most Australians live in this region.*

## POPULATION

**VERY CROWDED LANDS**

**CROWDED LANDS**

**LESS CROWDED LANDS**

**ALMOST EMPTY LANDS**

Most Australians live in the cities along the southeast coast. This is one of the areas with good farmland. City people call the huge, dry interior of Australia "the outback". The dry grasslands are used for raising sheep and cattle. Wool is a major export. Wheat is Australia's major crop.

Many unique animals, such as the kangaroo, koala and platypus, are found only here. Off the east coast lies the Great Barrier Reef. It's the largest coral reef in the world and is home to thousands of kinds of fish.

The original people of Australia are known as the Aborigines. Settlers from Great Britain began arriving over 200 years ago. Today, English is spoken and most people have a European heritage. Australia is Earth's only continent to have just one nation.

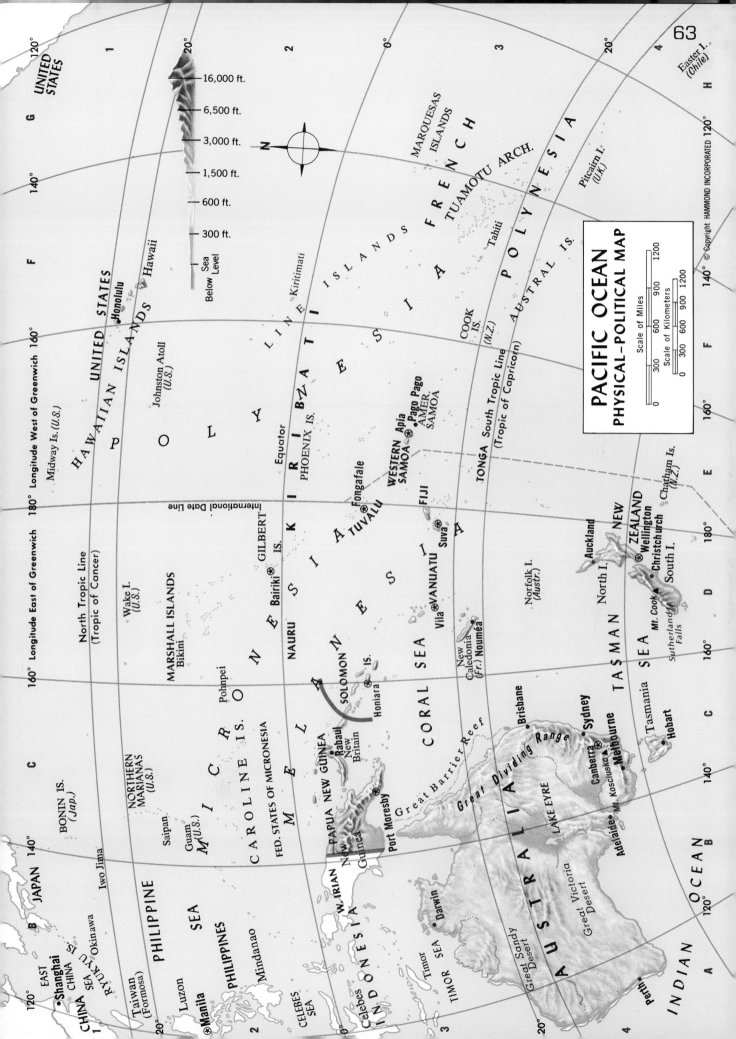

PACIFIC OCEAN
PHYSICAL-POLITICAL MAP

# AUSTRALIA

Many maps show New Zealand with Australia. This island nation lies southeast of Australia. Both North and South Islands, the two largest, have rugged mountains and a cool climate. The British also settled in New Zealand and English is spoken. Sheep are grazed and wool is the major export.

*Wheat is Australia's main agricultural product. It is grown on about half of Australia's farmland. Sheep-raising is another important occupation.*

**LEADING PRODUCTS**

**VEGETATION**

Look at the map on the previous page. When British settlers arrived in New Zealand, they found Maoris, a Polynesian people living there. Along with Melanesia and Micronesia, Polynesia makes up an area of the Pacific Ocean called **Oceania.** It is a vast area of small islands, many far from the next. It includes the Hawaiian Islands, the land of the fiftieth state of the United States.

## CONTINENT CLOSEUP

★ Nine of every ten Australians live in cities or towns.

★ Koalas are not bears. They are marsupials that feed on eucalyptus trees and shoots, and drink no water.

★ Edward Eyre was the first person to cross the continent in 1841.

★ Most of the Great Barrier Reef is a National Park. Taking coral from the reef is strictly forbidden.

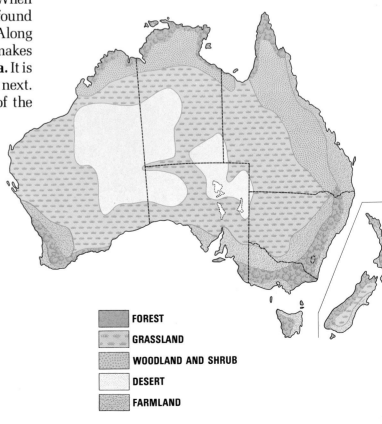

| | |
|---|---|
| ■ | FOREST |
| ▨ | GRASSLAND |
| ▦ | WOODLAND AND SHRUB |
| □ | DESERT |
| ▥ | FARMLAND |

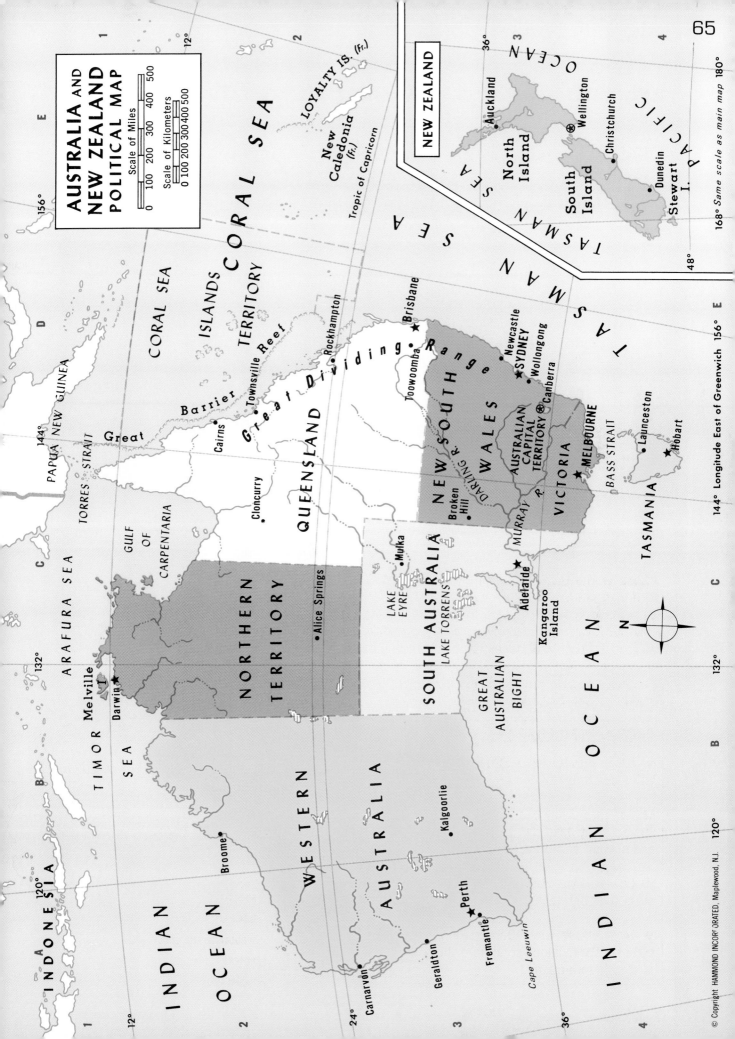

## AUSTRALIA AND NEW ZEALAND POLITICAL MAP

Scale of Miles
0 100 200 300 400 500

Scale of Kilometers
0 100 200 300 400 500

**NEW ZEALAND**

PACIFIC OCEAN

Auckland

North Island

Wellington ⊗

South Island

Christchurch

Dunedin

Stewart I.

TASMAN SEA

168° Same scale as main map 180°

36°

48°

LOYALTY IS. (Fr.)

New Caledonia (Fr.)

Tropic of Capricorn

CORAL SEA

CORAL SEA ISLANDS TERRITORY

Great Barrier Reef

Townsville

Cairns

Great

PAPUA NEW GUINEA

TORRES STRAIT

ARAFURA SEA

TIMOR SEA

Melville I.

Darwin ★

INDONESIA

INDIAN OCEAN

GULF OF CARPENTARIA

Rockhampton

Brisbane ★

Toowoomba

Great Dividing Range

QUEENSLAND

Cloncurry

NORTHERN TERRITORY

Alice Springs

WESTERN AUSTRALIA

Broome

Kalgoorlie

Geraldton

Carnarvon

Fremantle

Perth ★

Cape Leeuwin

GREAT AUSTRALIAN BIGHT

SOUTH AUSTRALIA

LAKE EYRE

LAKE TORRENS

Mulka

Kangaroo Island

Adelaide ★

Broken Hill

NEW SOUTH WALES

DARLING R.

MURRAY R.

Newcastle

SYDNEY ★

Wollongong

Canberra ⊗

AUSTRALIAN CAPITAL TERRITORY

VICTORIA

MELBOURNE ★

BASS STRAIT

Launceston

Hobart ★

TASMANIA

INDIAN OCEAN

N

156° E

144° Longitude East of Greenwich 156° E

132°

120°

12°

24°

36°

# ANTARCTICA: THE COLDEST CONTINENT

Antarctica is the southernmost continent on Earth. In size, Antarctica is smaller than South America, but larger than Europe. The southern edges of the Pacific, Atlantic and Indian Oceans surround Antarctica.

Many maps make Antarctica appear huge Look at the world map on pages 34-35. To show the round world on a flat map, some areas are distorted from their real shapes. Compare Antarctica on the map below. This map is a type of polar projection. It is centered on the South Pole, instead of the equator. On this map, the size and shape of Antarctica is truer to the way it actually is.

East Antarctica is a high plateau. Most of the western half of the continent is below sea level. The Antarctic Peninsula extends like a finger toward South America. Experts think the mountains here are an extension of the Andes range.

Very little of Antarctica's land can be seen. Ice and snow a mile thick covers the land. It is the coldest continent on Earth. There is more fresh water in this icecap than on all six other continents combined. Antarctica's climate is very dry.

Cold, bitter winds whip across the continent. In spring, icebergs break off from the edges of the icecap. Animals, such as seals and penguins, live at the coasts, feeding on fish. The climate is too cold for any food crops.

Antarctica has no permanent settlers. It is the last continent to be explored. A dozen nations have scientific stations here. Many nations are interested in the natural resources that may lie under Antarctica's frozen surface.

## CONTINENT CLOSEUP

★ In Wilkes Land, the icecap is more than three miles thick.

★ A Norwegian group, led by Roald Amundsen, was the first group to reach the South Pole, in 1911.

★ Whales migrate here in summer to feed on krill in the offshore waters.

★ Much of west Antarctica is below sea level. If the icecap melted, this area would be a chain of islands in a vast sea.

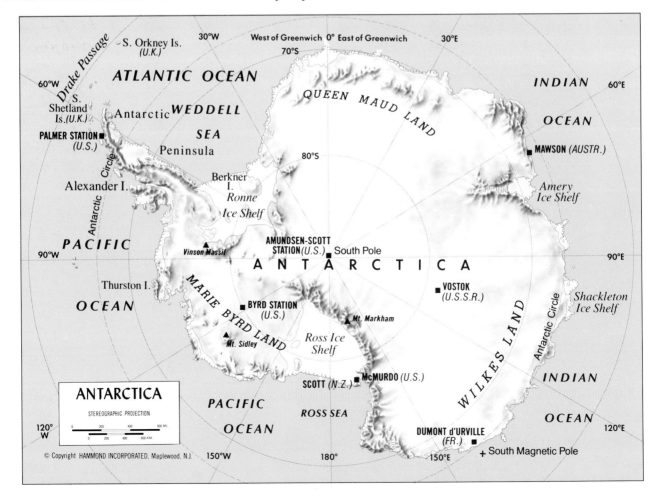

# CONTINENT COMPARISONS

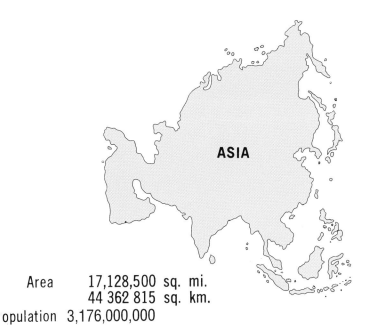

ASIA

Area    17,128,500 sq. mi.
        44 362 815 sq. km.
opulation  3,176,000,000

AFRICA

Area    11,707,000 sq. mi.
        30 321 130 sq. km.
Population  648,000,000

NORTH

AMERICA

Area    9,363,000 sq. mi.
        24 250 170 sq. km.
opulation  427,000,000

SOUTH

AMERICA

Area    6,875,000 sq. mi.
        17 806 250 sq. km.
Population  297,000,000

ANTARCTICA

Area    5,500,000 sq. mi.
        14 245 000 sq. km.
opulation  No permanent population

EUROPE

Area    4,057,000 sq. mi.
        10 507 630 sq. km.
Population  689,000,000

AUSTRALIA

Area    2,967,741 sq. mi.
        7 686 449 sq. km.
Population  17,288,000

# GEOGRAPHIC COMPARISONS

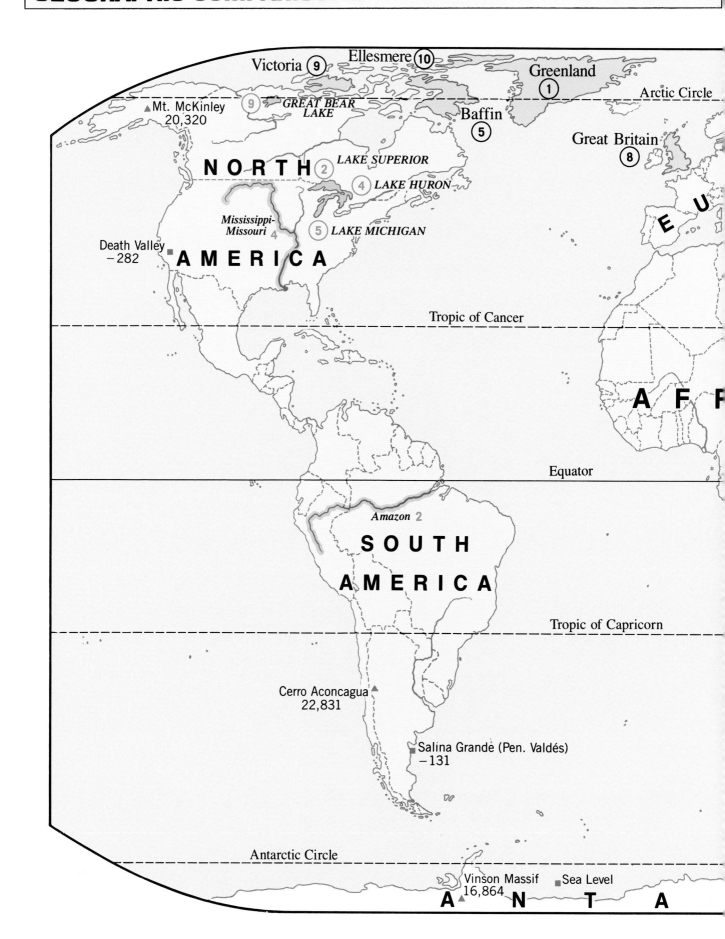

Victoria ⑨   Ellesmere ⑩   Greenland ①   Arctic Circle

▲ Mt. McKinley
20,320

⑨   *GREAT BEAR LAKE*

Baffin ⑤

Great Britain ⑧

**N O R T H**   ② *LAKE SUPERIOR*

④ *LAKE HURON*

E U

*Mississippi-
Missouri*   4

⑤ *LAKE MICHIGAN*

Death Valley
−282

**A M E R I C A**

Tropic of Cancer

A   F   R

Equator

*Amazon* 2

**S O U T H**

**A M E R I C A**

Tropic of Capricorn

Cerro Aconcagua ▲
22,831

Salina Grande (Pen. Valdés)
−131

Antarctic Circle

Vinson Massif   ■ Sea Level
▲ 16,864

A   N   T   A

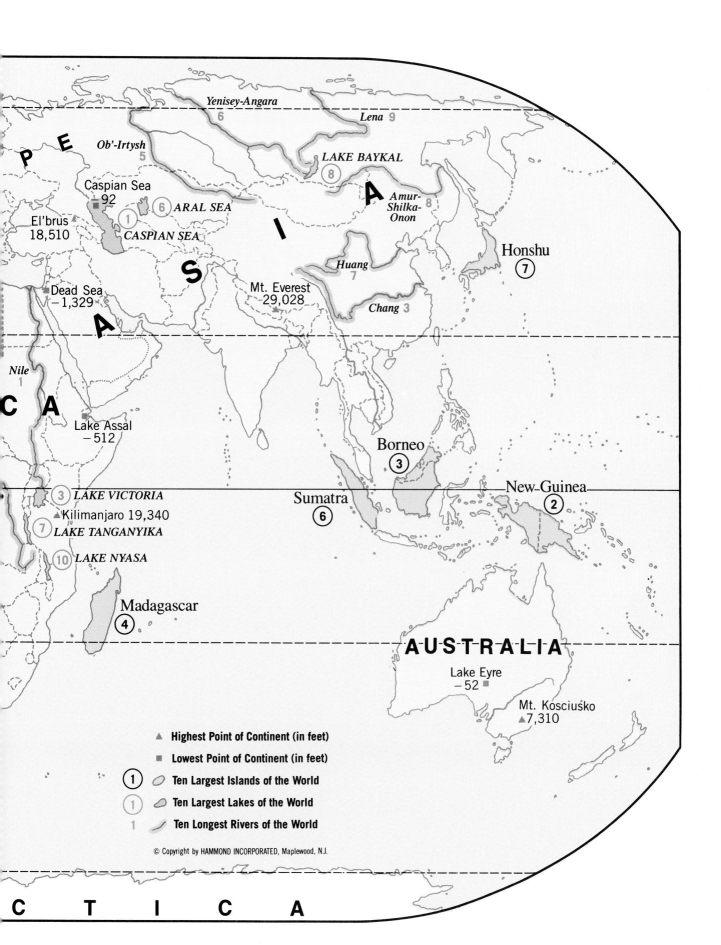

P E

Yenisey-Angara
6

Lena 9

Ob'-Irtysh
5

*LAKE BAYKAL*

Caspian Sea
−92

⑥ *ARAL SEA*

① *Amur-Shilka-Onon* 8

⑧

A S I A

El'brus
18,510

*CASPIAN SEA*

Honshu
⑦

*Huang*
7

Dead Sea
−1,329

Mt. Everest
29,028

*Chang* 3

C A

*Nile*
1

Lake Assal
−512

Borneo
③

Sumatra
⑥

New Guinea
②

③ *LAKE VICTORIA*

Kilimanjaro 19,340

⑦ *LAKE TANGANYIKA*

⑩ *LAKE NYASA*

Madagascar
④

A U S T R A L I A

Lake Eyre
−52

Mt. Kosciusko
7,310

▲ **Highest Point of Continent (in feet)**

■ **Lowest Point of Continent (in feet)**

① **Ten Largest Islands of the World**

① **Ten Largest Lakes of the World**

1 **Ten Longest Rivers of the World**

© Copyright by HAMMOND INCORPORATED, Maplewood, N.J.

C T I C A

# WHERE IN THE WORLD

| | HIGHEST PLACES | LOWEST PLACES | DRIEST PLACES |
|---|---|---|---|
| **NORTH AMERICA** | Mount McKinley, Alaska: 20,320 feet | Death Valley, California: 282 feet below sea level | Batagues, Mexico: one inch of rain a year |
| **SOUTH AMERICA** | Aconcagua, Argentina: 22,831 feet | Valdés Peninsula, Argentina: 131 feet below sea level | Atacama Desert, Chile: rain only two to four times a century |
| **AFRICA** | Kilimanjaro, Tanzania: 19,340 feet | Lake Assal, Djibouti: 512 feet below sea level | Wadi Halfa, Sudan: less than one-tenth of an inch of rain a year |
| **EUROPE** | Mount Elbrus, Russia: 18,510 feet | Caspian Sea, Russia: 92 feet below sea level | Astrakhan, Russia: six inches of rain a year |
| **ASIA** | Mount Everest, Nepal/China: 29,028 feet | Dead Sea, Israel/Jordan: 1,329 feet below sea level | Aden, Yemen: two inches of rain a year |
| **AUSTRALIA & THE PACIFIC** | Mauna Kea, Hawaii: 13,796 feet Mt. Kosciusko, Australia: 7,310 feet | Lake Eyre, Australia: 52 feet below sea level | Mulka, Australia: four inches of rain a year |
| **ANTARCTICA** | Vinson Massif: 16,864 feet | Unknown | South Pole Station: less than one inch of snow a year |

| WETTEST PLACES | WARMEST PLACES | COLDEST PLACES |
|---|---|---|
| Henderson Lake, Canada: 262 inches of rain a year | Death Valley, California: 134 degrees F., July 10, 1913 Yuma, Arizona: 108 degrees, average daily high in July | Northice, Greenland: -87 degrees F., Jan. 9, 1954 Eismitte, Greenland: -53 degrees, average daily low in January |
| Quibdo, Colombia: 354 inches of rain a year | Rivadavia, Argentina: 120 degrees F., Dec. 11, 1905 Santiago del Estero, Argentina: 97 degrees, average daily high in January | Sarmiento, Argentina: -27 degrees F., June 1, 1907 La Quiaca, Argentina: 16 degrees, average daily low in July |
| Debundscha, Cameroon: 405 inches of rain a year | Al'Aziziyah, Libya: 136 degrees F., Sept. 13, 1922 Adrar, Algeria: 115 degrees, average daily high in July | Ifrane, Morocco: -11 degrees F., Feb. 11, 1935 Tshabong, Botswana: 34 degrees, average daily low in July |
| Crkvica, Yugoslavia: 183 inches of rain a year | Seville, Spain: 122 degrees F., August 4, 1881 Seville, Spain: 97 degrees, average daily high in August | Ust'Shchugor, Russia: -67 degrees F., date unknown Ust'Shchugor, Russia: -14 degrees F., average daily low in January |
| Cherrapunji, India: 450 inches of rain a year | Tirat Zevi, Israel: 129 degrees F., June 21, 1942 Abadan, Iran: 112 degrees, average daily high in July | Verkhoyansk, Russia: -92 degrees F., June 21, 1942 Verkhoyansk, Russia: -63 degrees F., average daily low in January |
| Mount Waialeale, Hawaii: 460 inches of rain a year Tully, Australia: 179 inches of rain a year | Cloncurry, Australia: 128 degrees F., January 16, 1889 Mundiwindi, Australia: 101 degrees, average daily high in January | Charlotte Pass, Australia: -8 degrees F., July 22, 1947 Canberra, Australia: 33 degrees, average daily low in July |
| Unknown | Esperanza, Palmer Peninsula: 58 degrees F., October 20, 1956 | Vostok Station: -128 degrees F., July 21, 1983 |

*Temperatures shown in degrees Fahrenheit.*

# WHERE IN THE WORLD

| | LONGEST RIVERS | MAJOR LAKES | WATERFALLS |
|---|---|---|---|
| **NORTH AMERICA** | Mississippi-Missouri, United States: 3,710 miles | Superior, USA/Canada: 31,700 square miles<br>Huron, USA/Canada: 23,000 square miles<br>Michigan, USA: 22,300 square miles | Yosemite, California: 2,425-foot drop (3 steps)<br>Ribbon, California: 1,612-foot drop<br>Niagara, USA/Canada: 167-foot drop |
| **SOUTH AMERICA** | Amazon, Brazil/Peru: 4,000 miles | Maracaibo, Venezuela: 5,120 square miles | Angel, Venezuela: 3,212-foot drop (2 steps)<br>Cequenan, Venezuela: 2,000-foot drop<br>Iguaçu, Argentina/Brazil: 237-foot drop |
| **AFRICA** | Nile, Egypt/Sudan/ Uganda/Burundi: 4,145 miles | Victoria, Kenya/ Uganda/Tanzania: 26,820 square miles<br>Tanganyika, Burundi/ Zaire/Tanzania/Zambia: 12,350 square miles | Tugela, South Africa: 3,110-foot drop (5 steps)<br>Victoria, Zimbabwe/Zambia: 355-foot drop |
| **EUROPE** | Volga, Russia: 2,290 miles | Caspian Sea 143,240 square miles<br>Ladoga, Russia: 7,104 square miles | Kile, Norway: 1,840-foot drop (2 steps)<br>Gavarnie, France: 1,384-foot drop |
| **ASIA** | Chang Jiang (Yangtze), China: 3,965 miles | Caspian Sea 143,240 square miles<br>Aral Sea, Kazakhstan/Uzbekistan: 15,830 square miles<br>Baykal, Russia: 12,160 square miles | Jog, India: 830-foot drop<br>Khone, Laos: 70-foot drop |
| **AUSTRALIA & THE PACIFIC** | Murray-Darling, Australia: 2,310 miles | Eyre, Australia: 3,000 square miles | Sutherland, N. Z.: 1,904-foot drop (3 steps) |
| **ANTARCTICA** | | | |

| MAJOR ISLANDS | ACTIVE VOLCANOES |
|---|---|

**MAJOR ISLANDS**

| | |
|---|---|
| Greenland:<br>840,000 square miles | Ellesmere:<br>75,767 square miles |
| Baffin:<br>195,928 square miles | Newfoundland:<br>42,031 square miles |
| Victoria:<br>83,896 square miles | Cuba:<br>40,533 square miles |

Tierra del Fuego:
18,600 square miles
Marajó:
15,500 square miles

Madagascar:
226,400 square miles

| | |
|---|---|
| Great Britain:<br>84,400 square miles | Svalbard:<br>23,957 square miles |
| Iceland:<br>39,768 square miles | |
| Ireland:<br>31,743 square miles | |

| | |
|---|---|
| New Guinea:<br>305,000 square miles | Honshu:<br>88,000 square miles |
| Borneo:<br>290,000 square miles | Java:<br>48,842 square miles |
| Sumatra:<br>164,000 square miles | Luzon:<br>40,420 square miles |

| | |
|---|---|
| New Guinea:<br>305,000 square miles | Tasmania:<br>24,600 square miles |
| South Island, N. Z.:<br>58,393 square miles | New Britain:<br>14,600 square miles |
| North Island, N. Z.:<br>44,187 square miles | |

Alexander:
16,700 square miles

**ACTIVE VOLCANOES**

| | |
|---|---|
| Mt. St. Helens, Washington:<br>erupted in 1980 | El Chichon, Mexico:<br>erupted in 1982 |
| Mount Irazu, Costa Rica:<br>erupted in 1988 | Mount Redoubt,<br>Alaska:<br>erupted in 1989 |
| Izalco Volcano, El Salvador:<br>erupted in 1966 | |

Nevado del Ruiz, Colombia:
erupted in 1985
Cotopaxi, Ecuador:
erupted in 1975
Guagua Pichincha, Ecuador:
erupted in 1982

Cameroon Mountain, Cameroon:
erupted in 1986

| | |
|---|---|
| Mount Etna, Italy:<br>erupted in 1989 | Surtsey, Iceland:<br>erupted in 1987 |
| Stromboli, Italy:<br>erupted in 1989 | |
| Mount Vesuvius, Italy:<br>erupted in 1944 | |

| | |
|---|---|
| Mount Kelud, Indonesia:<br>erupted in 1967 | On-Take, Japan:<br>erupted in 1980 |
| Mount Kerinci, Indonesia:<br>erupted in 1987 | Klyuchevskaya<br>Sopka, Russia:<br>erupted in 1985 |
| Mount Pinatubo, Philippines:<br>erupted in 1991 | |

| | |
|---|---|
| Mauna Loa, Hawaii:<br>erupted in 1987 | Kilauea, Hawaii:<br>erupted in 1990 |
| Ruapehu, New Zealand:<br>erupted in 1989 | |
| Mount Ulawun, New Britain:<br>erupted in 1989 | |

Mount Erebus, Ross Island:
erupted in 1988
Big Ben, Heard Island:
erupted in 1986

# WHERE IN THE WORLD

| | REPTILES & AMPHIBIANS | | BIRDS | |
|---|---|---|---|---|
| **NORTH AMERICA** | Rattlesnakes<br>Corn Snake<br>Copperhead<br>Water Moccasin<br>Coral Snake<br>King Snake | Bullfrog<br>Box Turtle<br>Horned Lizard<br>Alligator<br>Gila Monster<br>Skink | Turkey<br>Mourning Dove<br>Canada Goose<br>Robin<br>Roadrunner<br>Burrowing Owl | Cardinal<br>Prairie Chicken<br>Wood Duck<br>Loon<br>Snowy Egret<br>Bald Eagle |
| **SOUTH AMERICA** | Boa Constrictor<br>Anaconda<br>Bushmaster<br>Fer-de-lance | Horned Frog<br>Galapagos Tortoise<br>Spectacled Caiman<br>Iguana<br>Surinam Toad | Rhea<br>Keel-billed Toucan<br>Cock-of-the-Rock<br>Hummingbird<br>Tinamou<br>Macaw | Potoo<br>Flamingo<br>Scarlet Ibis<br>Andean Condor<br>Hoatzin |
| **AFRICA** | Black Mamba<br>Rock Python<br>Ringhals (Spitting Cobra)<br>African Egg Eater<br>Gaboon Viper<br>Boomslang | Crocodile<br>Nile Monitor<br>Chameleon<br>Clawed Frog<br>Plated Lizard<br>Goliath Frog | Ostrich<br>Secretary Bird<br>Lanner Falcon<br>Vulture<br>Emerald Cuckoo<br>Shoebill | Flamingo<br>Touraco<br>Helmet Bird<br>Weaverbird<br>Oxpecker |
| **EUROPE** | Cross Adder<br>Grass Snake<br>Asp | Green Tree Frog<br>Pond Turtle<br>Alpine Newt<br>Fire Salamander<br>European Toad<br>Greek Tortoise | Skylark<br>White Stork<br>House Sparrow<br>Nightingale<br>Brambling<br>Wall Creeper | Imperial Eagle<br>Grey Wagtail<br>Blackcap<br>Ring Ouzel<br>Raven<br>Jay |
| **ASIA** | King Cobra<br>Tree Snake<br>Russell's Viper<br>Reticulated Python<br>Banded Krait | Komodo Dragon<br>Salt-water Crocodile<br>Gavial<br>Mandarin Newt<br>Hardun<br>Flying Dragon | Mandarin Duck<br>Golden Pheasant<br>Peacock<br>Fruit Dove<br>Brahminy Kite<br>Tailorbird | Rhinoceros Hornbill<br>Himalayan Monal<br>Red Jungle Fowl<br>Magpie<br>Sarus Crane |
| **AUSTRALIA & THE PACIFIC** | Tiger Snake<br>Taipan<br>Australian Brown Snake<br>Death Adder<br>Sea Snakes | Moloch Lizard<br>Frilled Lizard<br>Gecko<br>Bearded Dragon<br>Skink<br>White's Frog | Cockatoo<br>Emu<br>Kookaburra<br>Black Swan<br>Lyrebird | Budgerigar<br>Regent Bowerbird<br>Grey Butcherbird<br>Blue Wren |
| **ANTARCTICA** | Sea Snakes | | Storm Petrel<br>Emperor Penguin | Albatross<br>Skua |

| MAMMALS | | | TREES | | GEMS |
|---|---|---|---|---|---|
| Canadian Otter | Jack Rabbit | Chipmunk | Douglas Fir | Sequoia | Turquoise |
| Grizzly Bear | Raccoon | Bison | White Pine | Maple | Aquamarine |
| White-tailed Deer | Porcupine | Beaver | Magnolia | Hemlock | Jade |
| Bighorn Sheep | Caribou | Puma | Sweet Gum | Hickory | Tourmaline |
| Grey Squirrel | Coyote | Muskrat | Redwood | | Agate |
| Striped Skunk | | | | | Peridot |
| Brazilian Tapir | Guinea Pig | Jaguar | Jacaranda | Balsa | Diamond |
| Giant Armadillo | Vampire Bat | Ocelot | Mahogany | Cashew | Amethyst |
| Giant Anteater | Marmoset | Opossum | Brazil Nut | Southern | Tourmaline |
| Two-toed Sloth | Capuchin | Llama | Logwood | Beech | Aquamarine |
| Chinchilla | | | | | Emerald |
| | | | | | Topaz |
| | | | | | Onyx |
| Hippopotamus | African Elephant | Baboon | Yellow-wood | Rosewood | Diamond |
| Rhinoceros | Honey Badger | Impala | Date Palm | Baobab | Emerald |
| Chimpanzee | Wart Hog | Lemur | African Tulip | Cedar | Tourmaline |
| Giraffe | Cheetah | Zebra | Cork Oak | Ebony | Garnet |
| Dromedary (Camel) | Lion | Hyena | Mangrove | Oil Palm | |
| Gorilla | | | | | |
| Red Deer | Mouflon | | Chestnut | Pine | Topaz |
| House Mouse | Weasel | | Juniper | Beech | Garnet |
| Wild Boar | Moose | | Walnut | Yew | |
| Red Fox | Chamois | | Cork Oak | Plain | |
| Reindeer | | | Spruce | Oak | |
| Indian Elephant | Mongoose | Leopard | Eastern Spruce | Sandalwood | Diamond |
| Bactrian Camel | Gibbon | Wolf | Rhododendron | Banyan | Ruby |
| Orangutan | Yak | Tiger | Cherry | Larch | Emerald |
| Rhesus Monkey | Blackbuck | Sable | Mango | Teak | Jade |
| Water Buffalo | Giant Panda | Lemming | Mulberry | Rubber | Zircon |
| | | | | | Sapphire |
| | | | | | Moonstone |
| Tasmanian Devil | Wombat | | Eucalyptus | Snow Gum | Sapphire |
| Duck-billed Platypus | Koala | | White Mallee | Silk Oak | Opal |
| Kangaroo | Dingo | | Wattle | Desert | Pearl |
| | | | Blue Gum | Kurrajong | |
| Sea Lion | Whales | | | | |

# WHERE IN THE WORLD

| | PRINCIPAL CITIES | LANDMARKS FROM THE PAST |
|---|---|---|
| **NORTH AMERICA** | New York, New York<br>Mexico City, Mexico<br>Los Angeles, California<br>Chicago, Illinois<br>Philidelphia, Pennsylvania<br>Toronto, Canada | Pyramid of the Moon, Teotihuacán,<br>   Mexico: built in 900–1100<br>Anasazi Pueblo Bonito,<br>   New Mexico: built about 1050<br>Chichén Itzá,<br>   Mexico: abandoned in 1400s |
| **SOUTH AMERICA** | São Paulo, Brazil<br>Buenos Aires, Argentina,<br>Rio de Janiero, Brazil<br>Caracas, Venezuela<br>Bogotá, Colombia<br>Lima, Peru | Royal Road of the Incas, Andes<br>   Mountains: built in 1200–1500<br>Machu Picchu,<br>   Peru: built in 1200–1500<br>Chan Chan,<br>   Peru: built in 1000–1400 |
| **AFRICA** | Cairo, Egypt<br>Lagos, Nigeria<br>Johannesburg, South Africa | The Sphinx and Giza Pyramids,<br>   Egypt: begun about 2500 B.C.<br>Temple of Ramses II,<br>   Egypt: built about 1250 B.C.<br>Great Zimbabwe ruins,<br>   Zimbabwe: built in 1000–1400 |
| **EUROPE** | London, England   Milan, Italy<br>Paris, France   Rome, Italy<br>Moscow, Russia   Athens, Greece<br>Berlin, Germany   Istanbul, Turkey<br>St. Petersburg, Russia<br>Madrid, Spain | Acropolis of Athens,<br>   Greece: begun in 400s B.C.<br>Colosseum of Rome,<br>   Italy: begun about 70 B.C.<br>Stonehenge ruins, England:<br>   built 1800-1400 B.C. |
| **ASIA** | Tokyo, Japan   Jakarta, Indonesia<br>Shanghai, China   Bombay, India<br>Beijing, China   Manila, Philippines<br>Calcutta, India   Karachi, Pakistan<br>Seoul, Korea   Bangkok, Thailand<br>Taipei, Taiwan   Tehran, Iran | Great Wall of China:<br>   begun about 200 B.C.<br>Dome of the Rock,<br>   Jerusalem: begun in 691<br>Taj Mahal,<br>   India: built in 1600s |
| **AUSTRALIA & THE PACIFIC** | Sydney, Australia<br>Melbourne, Australia<br>Honolulu, Hawaii | Caves of Uluru, or Ayers Rock,<br>   Australia: dates unknown<br>Giant Statues,<br>   Easter Island: origin unknown |
| **ANTARCTICA** | | |

| MODERN ENGINEERING MARVELS | | TALLEST BUILDINGS |
|---|---|---|
| Delaware Tunnel, New York State, USA: 105-mile water tunnel, world's longest tunnel<br>CN Tower, Toronto, Canada: 1,815-foot tower with revolving restaurant | Panama Canal, Panama: 51-mile waterway, opened 1914, connects Atlantic and Pacific<br>Lake Pontchartrain Causeway, Louisiana, USA: 24 miles long, world's longest bridge | Sears Tower, Chicago, Illinois: 1,454 feet<br>World Trade Center, New York, N. Y.: 1,350 feet<br>Empire State Building, New York, N. Y.: 1,250 feet |
| Itaipu Hydroelectric Dam, Paraná River, Brazil/Paraguay: world's largest waterpower project | | Parque Central Torre Officinas, Caracas, Venezuela: 656 feet |
| Lake Volta, Ghana: 3,275 square miles, world's largest artificial lake<br>Kimberley Mine, South Africa: over 3000-foot deep, 1500-foot wide pit. world's largest excavation | Aswan High Dam, Nile River, Egypt: over two-and-a-half miles long, 364 feet high<br>Suez Canal, Egypt: opened 1869 100 miles long, connects Red and Mediterranean Seas | Carlton Centre, Johannesburg, South Africa: 722 feet |
| Volga-Baltic Waterway, Russia: 1,850 miles long, world's longest canal system<br>National TV Tower, Plock, Poland: 2,120 feet tall, world's tallest structure | Humber Bridge, England: 4,626 foot suspension span<br>Eiffel Tower, Paris, France: 1,052 feet tall, opened 1889<br>Channel Tunnel, England/France: world's longest undersea tunnel | Palace of Science and Culture, Warsaw, Poland: 790 feet<br>Moscow State University, Moscow, Russia: 787 feet<br>Maine Montparnasse, Paris, France: 751 feet |
| Akashi-Kaikyo Bridge, Japan: 5,840-foot suspension span, world's longest single span<br>Seikan Rail Tunnel, Japan: 33 miles world's longest | Rogun Dam, Vakhsh River, Tajikistan: 1,066 feet tall, world's highest dam | Sunshine Sixty, Tokyo, Japan: 787 feet<br>Ikebukuro Office Tower, Tokyo, Japan: 742 feet |
| Trans-Australian Railroad, Australia: 298 miles of straight track in one stretch | | MLC Centre, Sydney, Australia: 800 feet<br>Rialto Tower, Melbourne, Australia: 794 feet |
| | | |

# WHERE IN THE WORLD

| | FOOD SPECIALTIES |
|---|---|
| **NORTH AMERICA** | Barbados: Cou-cou (cornmeal and okra)<br>Jamaica: Jerk Pork (cured pork strips)<br>Mexico: Tortillas (corn pancakes) and Tamales (cornmeal and meat)<br>Panama: Guacho (rice and beans)<br>USA: Fried Chicken and Cheeseburgers |
| **SOUTH AMERICA** | Argentina: Asado con Cuero (barbecued beef)<br>Bolivia: Humitas (corn pies)<br>Brazil: Feijoada (rice, black beans, meat and manioc)<br>Chile: Empanada (beef turnover)<br><br>Colombia: Ajiaco (vegetable soup)<br>Paraguay: Puchero (beef and vegetable stew)<br>Venezuela: Hallaca (cornmeal and meat cooked in banana leaves) |
| **AFRICA** | Egypt: Felafel (ground chickpeas and beans)<br>Ethiopia: Wat (spicy meat and vegetable stew)<br>Morocco: Bastila (pigeon pie)<br>Northern Africa: Couscous (steamed semolina) and Brik (fried meat turnover cooked with egg)<br><br>Southern Africa: Bredi (lamb and pumpkin stew) and Mealies (corn porridge)<br>Sudan: Ful (oil-cooked beans)<br>Western Africa: Fufu (ground cassava in sauce) and Peanut Soup |
| **EUROPE** | Austria: Schnitzel (breaded veal cutlet)<br>England: Yorkshire Pudding (meat drippings)<br>France: Bouillabaisse (fish-based soup)<br>Germany: Sauerbraten (marinated pot roast)<br>Greece: Moussaka (eggplant, lamb and custard)<br>Hungary: Goulash (paprika-spiced beef stew)<br><br>Italy: Pasta (noodles)<br>Poland: Pierogi (filled dumpling)<br>Romania: Mamaliga (corn bread or mush)<br>Scotland: Haggis (boiled lamb pudding)<br>Spain: Paella (chicken, fish and rice)<br>Sweden: Smorgasbord (cold buffet) |
| **ASIA** | China: Won Ton (stuffed dumpling)<br>India: Curries (seasoned dishes)<br>Indonesia: Nasi Goreng (rice and side dishes)<br>Japan: Sashimi (raw fish)<br>Korea: Kimchi (fermented cabbage and fish)<br>Malaysia: Rendang (coconut milk beef stew)<br><br>Middle East: Kibbeh (ground wheat and lamb) and Shish Kebab (skewered meat and vegetables)<br>Philippines: Adobo (chicken and pork in soy and vinegar sauce)<br>Turkey: Baklava (honey and nut pastry) |
| **AUSTRALIA & THE PACIFIC** | Australia: Pavlova (kiwi meringue pie) and Vegemite (yeast spread)<br>New Zealand: Toheroa (green clam soup)<br>Polynesia: Poi (ground taro root) |
| **ANTARCTICA** | |

## PRINCIPAL CROPS

| | | |
|---|---|---|
| Wheat | Tobacco | Corn |
| Oranges | Peanuts | Oats |
| Sugar Beets | Potatoes | Grapes |
| Soybeans | Apples | |
| Cotton | Peaches | |

| | | |
|---|---|---|
| Coffee | Maize | Rice |
| Bananas | Soybeans | Wheat |
| Sugarcane | Cacao Beans | Nuts |
| Cassava | Oranges | Grapes |

| | | |
|---|---|---|
| Cassava | Cacao Beans | Yams |
| Sugarcane | Cotton | Olives |
| Plantains | Dates | Grapes |
| Millet | Palm Oil | Rice |
| Bananas | Oranges | |

| | | |
|---|---|---|
| Potatoes | Tomatoes | Oats |
| Sugar Beets | Maize | Oranges |
| Wheat | Apples | Rye |
| Barley | Cabbage | Flax |
| Grapes | Olives | |

| | | |
|---|---|---|
| Coconuts | Jute | Tea |
| Sugarcane | Rubber | Wheat |
| Rice | Millet | Cotton |
| Palm Oil | Spices | Onions |
| Sweet Potatoes | Maize | |

| | | |
|---|---|---|
| Wheat | Oats | |
| Sugarcane | Apples | |
| Barley | Oranges | |

## ORIGINS OF SPORTS

| | |
|---|---|
| Baseball: Northeast USA, 1840s | Lacrosse: Canada, date unknown |
| Basketball: Springfield, Massachusetts: 1891 | Football: United States, late 1860s |
| Volleyball: Holyoke, Massachusetts, 1895 | Ice Hockey: Canada, 1850s |

| | |
|---|---|
| Bowling: Egypt, as early as 5200 B.C. | |
| Boxing: Egypt, 4000 B.C. | |

| | |
|---|---|
| Bobsledding: Switzerland, 1889 | Tennis: France, around 1100 |
| Track and Field: Greece, Ireland, before 1300 B.C. | Golf: Scotland, 1450s |
| Alpine Skiing: Norway, 1843 | Cricket: England, late 1300s |

| | |
|---|---|
| Wrestling: Iraq (Sumeria), 2600 B.C. | Soccer: China, around 200 B.C. |
| Swimming: Japan, 1600s | |
| Polo: Iran (Persia), as early as 2000 B.C. | |

| | |
|---|---|
| Australian Rules Football: Ballarat, Australia, 1853 | |

# MAP INDEX (Selected Names)

**Dear Parents and Readers:**

Throughout **Discovering Maps,** many questions are asked to encourage our young readers to think about what they have just read. In doing so, we hope our readers will acquire a better understanding of the concepts in this introduction to maps.

Everyone likes to be assured that the answer they've come up with is the correct one. To help you out, we've provided answers in two sections. The first contains specific answers to the feature questions, "Think About It". A second section contains some of the answers to questions raised in the text.

### Answers to Think About It:

Page 4: 1. Model airplanes, cars, a dollhouse, a stuffed toy animal or a model farm are some of the possible answers.
2. A globe is *like* a picture of the Earth because it is round; they both have land and water; both land and water are different colors; the shapes of the land on a globe are the same as in the picture.
A globe is *different* because it gives the names of places; a globe has no clouds to obscure the view; it may or may not be larger or smaller than the picture.

Page 5: You can only see half of Earth at one time because a globe is round. When you see one side, the other side is hidden.

Page 6: 1. You would live in Hawaii, the only state of the United States that is not part of North America.
2. Your location changes when you go from home to school or to the store. But, you usually remain in your city, state, country, continent and hemisphere. Unless you are an astronaut, you always remain on the same planet.

Page 7: Twelve hours.

Page 8 (top): Each year has an extra ¼ day. Every four years we usually add that extra day.

Page 8 (bottom): 1. Among the effects: the northern half of Earth gets more light and heat because the sun is shining more directly (it is higher in the sky) and there are more hours of daylight.
2. The North Pole leans away from the sun in December.

Page 9: 1. Yes, most of the United States is in a region of Earth where seasons change.
2. The same number of revolutions as your age in years.

Page 11: 1. *Alike:* The map and photo show the same area, location and shapes.
*Differ:* The map shows less detail. Objects on the map are not obstructed by shadows or trees. The map has a key to help identify types of things such as buildings, roads and walkways. Names are shown on the map but not in the photo.
2. The map tells you the names of buildings, shows what areas are parks, gives you the names of streets and helps you tell how far apart these things are.

Page 12: 1-c, 2-e, 3-d, 4-b, 5-a.

Page 13: 1. Blue, purple, white or grey.
2. Red, orange or yellow.
3. Yellow, brown.
4. Brown, purple, white, green or black.

Page 15: 1. The North Pole. The bear is probably a polar bear and would be white.
2. SE and NW.
3. a: northeast; b: southwest; c: northwest; d: southeast.

Page 17: 1. 250 miles.
2. No, they are divided by Lake Michigan.
3. The road distance would be longer than a straight line on a map, because roads curve as they follow the shape of the land.

Page 18: 1. 100 miles
2. 300 miles
3. 400 miles
4. 200 miles
5. 250 miles

Page 19: Dover, Delaware, C-3
Annapolis, Maryland, B-4
Trenton, New Jersey, D-2
Harrisburg, Pennsylvania, B-2

Page 22: 1. 30° N, 90° W
2. Washington, D.C.
3. Thirty degrees

Page 23: 1. Hawaii
2. 7:00 P.M. Eastern Time
3. a. 1:00 P.M.
b. 2:00 P.M.
c. 3:00 P.M.
d. 11:00 A.M.
e. 10:00 A.M.
4. 8:00 A.M. Monday

Page 24: 1. Larger
2. Hawaii is farthest south. Note the latitude lines that pass through Hawaii and Florida.
3. Alaska. The Aleutian islands extend past 180° W.

Page 25: 1. There are no boundary lines drawn in the ground, as on a map. You could see the boundary if it were the same as a river, or if you saw one of the many stone markers that surveyors have laid to show where boundaries are.
2. You might see a sign welcoming you to the state you just entered, or you may cross a river that you know is the boundary line between states.
3. When crossing an international boundary, you would usually encounter a customs post on the border. Some countries have visible barriers, such as fences, at their borders.

Page 27: 1. You would probably build a road across mountains at a low point, such as a pass. A seaport city would need a good harbor on a bay or inlet, or at the mouth of a river. A bridge or tunnel could be used to cross a river or other narrow body of water. Narrow mountains often have tunnels through them. Railroads usually follow the natural contours of the land, so they would most likely be built where the land is least steep.

2. Vacation resorts might be found along a sea-coast, near a waterfall or other such point of interest, or in the mountains, where it is cool in the summer and skiing might be available in the winter.

Page 29:  1. Elevation is measured from sea level. The base of Pikes Peak is on a plateau that is over a mile above sea level.

2. On a relief map, mountains look wrinkled. On a contour map, steep ground is shown where contour lines are closest together.

3. It would show where land would be low, flat and easy to cross, and where it would be steep and hard to climb. It would also show streams, lakes and swamps that you might have to hike around.

Page 31:  1. The interstate highway would probably be quickest, because it would probably have a higher speed limit, allowing you to travel faster.

2. Between Florida and California, I-10 passes through Alabama, Mississippi, Louisiana, Texas, New Mexico and Arizona.

Page 32:  Knowing the resources of a country might tell you what types of work you could expect to be available. You would be able to tell ahead of time which foods and manufactured products might be available at low cost because they were produced locally. You would be able to tell which products might not be readily available and might cost more if they were imported.

Page 33:  Most of the very crowded areas are near good farmland or along the coasts and major waterways. This allows large numbers of people to have food readily available. Few people live in desert lands that produce little or no food.

## Answers to Text Questions:

Page 4:  Land and water are different colors. Water is usually blue in photographs. The Earth looks small because it was photographed from very far away.

Page 5:  The four oceans are the Atlantic Ocean, Pacific Ocean, Indian Ocean and Arctic Ocean. Only 29 percent of Earth's surface is land; 71 percent is water.

Page 6:  The Indian Ocean does not touch North America.

Page 8:  Summer starts in the Southern Hemisphere on December 21 or 22.

Page 13:  Important roads are shown in red. So are mileages, so map readers can tell distances quickly.

Page 14:  Southeast is between south and east. Northwest is between north and west. If you traveled east all the way around the world, you would end up right back where you started.

Page 15:  To get from Montana to Illinois, you would travel southeast. In our example, the correct guess is Maryland.

Page 16:  It's almost one inch from Miami to Atlanta ($^{15}/_{16}$). That stands for almost 600 miles. The distance from Springfield to Harrisburg is 680 to 700 miles; from New York to Boston is 200 miles; from Dallas to New Orleans is 400 miles; from Chicago to Atlanta is 600 miles.

Page 18:  Cleveland is 50 miles from Canton on both maps. The scales are different.

Page 19:  Harrisburg is the capital of Pennsylvania. Erie is in square A-1, Pittsburgh is in A-3, and Philadelphia, Pennsylvania's largest city, is in D-4. To go from Dover to Bridgeport, you travel northeast.

Page 20:  The South Pole is 90 degrees south latitude or 90° S.

Page 23:  The Earth has 24 standard time zones. There are a number of areas that keep non-standard time. When you enter a time zone going from east to west, it becomes one hour earlier.

Page 25:  Ottawa is the capital of Canada. Mexico City is located at 20° N, 100° W. Washington, D.C. is near 40° N, 75° W. Alabama, Georgia and Mississippi are the three states that have the 35th parallel (35° N) as their northern boundary.

Page 28:  North America's highest land is in the west.

Page 29:  California's largest valley is in the middle of the state. Its highest mountains are in the east. The mountain shown on the contour map is over 3000 feet in elevation.

Page 30:  Interstate or limited access highways, federal (U.S.) and state highways are shown.

Page 31:  It's 118 miles from Gila Bend to Yuma. To go from Busch Gardens to the Sun Coast Dome, you would take Interstate 275, crossing the Howard Franklin Bridge. U.S. 92 is the route from Tampa International Airport across the Gandy Bridge. The Courtney Campbell Causeway takes you across Old Tampa Bay, as you travel the 22 miles from Tampa International Airport to Clearwater. The road from Clearwater to Treasure Island is a combination of state route 60 and state route 699, or a combination of state (Florida) routes 697 and 699. Treasure Island is named twice on the map; once for the island and once for the town of the same name. The London Wax Museum is nearby.

Page 32:  Food resources shown are bananas, citrus fruit, corn and vegetables. Cotton is a resource used to make clothing. The eastern half of the United States is more crowded. The northeast has more people than the northwest. No one lives on the far northern islands of North America.

Page 33:  More cities are found in crowded areas, fewer in less densely populated areas. Cities often offer higher paying jobs, more variety of jobs, and have more places to go, people to see and things to do.